The Church

A Discipleship Manual *for* The Body of Christ

R.P. Amos

Everyday Publications Inc.
310 Killaly St. W.
Port Colborne ON L3K 6A6
Canada

ISBN 978-0-88873-083-1

Cover Design:
Rachel Brooks

Printed in Canada

Introduction

This study manual is designed for disciples of the Lord Jesus Christ who are serious about serving Him. It deals with the subject of God's **church** and answers, from the Word of God, many questions Christians ask concerning the assembly (church) of God's New Testament children.

It is impossible to be a faithful disciple of the Lord and ignore His true church. For a disciple is a learner and follower of the Lord Jesus, who is the Head of the church.

With countless varieties of churches existing today, we ask the question, Does our living God still have a blueprint or pattern for His church? The answer is, ***absolutely yes!***

In the Old Testament, Moses was told to make the tabernacle (house of God) after the *"pattern"* God showed him in the mountain. But Hebrews 9:10,11 tells us that it only stood *"until the time of reformation"* which was the time of the cross-work of our Lord Jesus Christ. However, we are told that the old was a *"figure"* of a new and more perfect tabernacle which Christ has made without hands, i.e., it is a spiritual building. And so, the old way pictured a **specific** spiritual design to the gospel of Jesus Christ and His house today – the church – His children by grace alone.

As disciples, we are to base our actions and beliefs on the written Word of God – our beliefs as to the gospel we have trusted, who Jesus is, moral absolutes, etc. Why is it, though, that so many feel, when it comes to the church, it suddenly becomes optional how to do it? Why do people believe that man's modern ideas plus centuries of tradition can be more successful than God's pattern? If God has revealed truth for the church, why shouldn't that be obeyed also in simple faith?

Thus, this manual will deal with the operation of the church and how a disciple functions within it – according to the authority of the holy Word of God alone.

In writing this manual, by the grace of God, I am not representing any one system of Christian churches, for no group is perfect and free from man-made tradition in every respect. Although I frequent assemblies of Christians who practice much of what is taught in this manual from the Bible, I am committed to presenting the truth as found in the Holy Scriptures alone. My goal is to simply look at the Bible and with the Spirit's power communicate what He says. *Nothing more and nothing less.* If it cuts across man's tradition, so be it.

> *"He that hath an ear, let him hear what the Spirit saith unto the churches."* Rev. 2:7

Much of the material will be presented in outline form with many Bible verses given but not entirely printed out. It will be your responsibility to look these verses up in their proper context. All Scripture quotations are from the KJV translation. Upon completing your study, you should have a solid understanding of God's church and the disciple. However, if you have further questions regarding the truth presented, you may get in touch with me at the address on the last page.

Love in Christ Jesus the Lord,

R.P. Amos

Contents

Section 1

God's Church: His Representation on Earth

The Disciple's Mission

Because of what Satan, hypocrites, and tradition have done to the word 'church', do not under-estimate the value and importance of the true church. It means everything to the Lord Jesus Christ. Does Christ and His church mean everything to you?

Following are a few thoughts of what the Lord Jesus thinks of His church.

Acts 20:28	"*...the* **church** *of God, which He hath* ***purchased with His own blood.*"**
Eph. 5:25	"*...Christ also* ***loved*** *the* **church**, *and gave Himself for it.*"
Eph. 5:29	"*...but nourisheth and* ***cherisheth*** *it, even as the Lord the* **church**."
Eph. 5:31,32	"*...and they shall be* ***one flesh****. This is a great mystery: but I speak concerning* **Christ and the church**."

Yes, Christ and the church is a combination that can never be separated and this combination is the living God's master design in this world today. God asks the question in 1 Corinthians 11:22: ***"...Despise ye the church of God?"*** If your answer is no, then your response should be as Hebrews 10:25 says: *"Not forsaking the assembling of ourselves together..."*

The Birthday of the Church

The church of Jesus Christ has only existed on earth since the 50th day after His crucifixion. Before that, God worked through His chosen nation of Israel. But now He has opened His saving grace to the whole world. Acts chapters 1 and 2 record the beginning, setting, and birthday of the church. It involved three major actions.

#1. An Upward Action ↑

After spending about 33 years on the earth and then dying for sin on the cross, the Lord Jesus rose from the dead 3 days later in living power. Then for 40 days He instructed and commissioned His disciples to spread the gospel. Then He supernaturally left planet Earth, ascending from the Mount of Olives into the very heaven of God the Father. The promise in Acts 1:11 says that He will come back again someday. Although the Lord Jesus was now physically absent, His mission on earth did not end. Rather, the stage was set for a dynamic plan.

#2. A Downward Action ↓

A few days after the Lord's Ascension into heaven and exactly the 50th day from crucifixion (Jewish Feast of Weeks, Pentecost, while the high priest was waving to God two loaves of leavened bread being the first fruits of the harvest), the Lord Jesus kept His promise and sent down the Holy Spirit into His believing disciples. **God the Spirit was now replacing God the Son on earth.**

The day the Holy Spirit came down from heaven to live in believers was the day God's church (the assembly of Spirit-indwelt believers) was born. The assembly-church was now God's new representation on earth. These Spirit-born believers would be the Lord's living house on earth. He would live in this living house and He would operate out of it. 1 Timothy 3:15 says it this way: *"the house of God, which is the* ***church*** *of the living God."*

#3. An Outward Action →

The rest of the book of Acts relates how these empowered believers, with Jesus now living in them, went outward from Jerusalem into all the world with His saving gospel. When sinners repented and believed, they were structured into Christian assemblies in their respective cities. These church-assemblies became the controlled centers out of which God's Son would now be worshiped, His rule would be in effect, His children would learn and grow, and His gospel would be established.

As a believer in the Lord Jesus Christ, you should be involved with the greatest living organism on earth, the local assembly of Christians. Give yourself to the Lord of the church 100% through a Scriptural local assembly. His church has survived almost 2000 years because of its master design. God's spiritual workings, even in modern times, do not center in politics, social reforms, schools, sports, religion, etc., but in His church. As we serve our Lord today, can it be said of us as it was of Phebe in Romans 16:1: *"a **servant of the church** which is at"* ____________ (your city)?

The vast bulk of the New Testament (N.T.) is committed to planting (formation), maintaining order, governing, holy lifestyle, worship, and doctrine of the churches of Christ. Have you ever noticed that not one N.T. epistle (including Revelation) is addressed to the unsaved? Each letter is written to the saints (born again believers) and local churches of believers. **The local assembly is God's masterpiece and His power tool in the world today.** Do not make the mistake of building Christ's church around your private life (home, family, job, school, etc.), but build your private life around Christ and His church. ***"Seek ye first the kingdom of God,"*** Matt. 6:33.

The Lord Jesus said over 1900 years ago, *"I will build my church and the gates of hell shall not prevail against it,"* Matt. 16:18. Because of its superior design, the church has marched on with its mission and has survived the many severe attacks of Satan. Satan has made some inroads into it, but he hasn't won and will not win. Christ and the church – He and it, still live today!

Section 2

Beware of the Counterfeit Church

The Disciple's Enemy

Just as anything that's valuable is worth counterfeiting to some, so is the church in the spiritual warfare. 2 Corinthians 11 and Revelation 17 teach that Satan, God's arch-enemy, has counterfeited the Lord's true church.

WARNING Satan tries to confuse and mislead so as to prevent salvation, worship, and service to God in the right way. Some religions are cleverly disguised and appear outwardly holy, doing a good social work. *But, beware!!* For because of wolves in sheep's clothing, Matt. 7:15, not every building that has the name 'Christian' or 'Church' or has a cross on it is His real church.

One of the greatest illusions of some counterfeit churches is their reading of the Bible. This makes them appear to be of God. However, the majority of passages they read are instructions for born again believers on how to live the Christian life. These false churches do not dwell on the fact that **every** person is a hell deserving sinner, and only if he is born again spiritually by personal faith in the gospel of Jesus Christ **alone** will God consider him a real Christian. Millions of people are being told how to live like Christians without ever realizing three vital things:

#1. They are not true Christians.

#2. They must be born again by the Spirit of God to become true Christians.

#3. Only by the power of the indwelling Holy Spirit can one live the Christian life.

Example – It's similar to owning a bicycle, but reading a jet plane manual to learn how to fly the bike. You might pick up knowledge, but you'll never fly because the power isn't there.

Yes, the Bible warns believers so we will be aware of Satan who comes disguised as religious teachers preaching "*another* ***Jesus***," "*another* ***gospel***," and "*another* ***Spirit***," 2 Cor. 11:4.

The Lord's warning	***Beware!***	Matt. 7:15
The Lord's counsel	***Search the Scriptures***	John 5:39
The Lord's invitation	***Come unto me***	Matt. 11:28
The Lord's command	***Come out...separate***	2 Cor. 6:17

Following is a list of some major distinctions between the true church and the deadly imposter:

DIFFERENCES

The True Church	*The Counterfeit*
Has no particular name.	*Has many names – some are poor counterfeits and many are good counterfeits.*
Preaches that Christ's shed blood on the cross, plus nothing, is enough to pay for all one's sins by faith alone in the Lord Jesus Christ.	*Acknowledges that Christ died for sins and then blatantly proclaims that one must do certain rituals and works to pay for their own sins.*
Proclaims Jesus Christ as the one way to heaven and the only way to be in His church, which is His body.	*Reverses the truth and proclaims the church as the way to Christ and heaven.*
Proclaims the bodily resurrection of Christ proving He is Lord, intercessor, and great High Priest, thus able to keep one saved forever.	*Proclaims He is possibly alive, but then points members to some clergy-priests who will intercede for their sins.*
Proclaims judgment ahead for the world.	*Proclaims peace ahead for the world.*

Proclaims the Lord Jesus is coming back again – bodily.	*Proclaims a mixture of theories – that He has come back in Spirit or in the mystical sacraments, etc.*
Believes the Word of God, the Bible, as its only authority.	*Talks about the sacredness of the Bible but then obeys the traditions of men.*
Proclaims man's problem is his sinful heart, which must be changed through the Spirit.	*Proclaims the problem is man's outward environment, which, if changed through social reform or psychological formula, can be remedied.*
Tells believers not to be conformed to this world but to be transformed into the likeness of Jesus Christ.	*Encourages members by example to enjoy the pleasures of this present world.*
Only attraction is the unseen Lord Jesus, as it teaches the Word of God which is the sword of the Spirit.	*Attracts members with holy sanctuaries, crosses, relics, religious clothing, holy rituals, impressive titles for its clergy, entertaining programs, etc. — things which make one* ***feel*** *holy.*
Guides believers on a love and grace principle.	*Controls members by a system of fear and religious works.*
Walks by the unseen, by faith in His promises.	*Walks by sight – some use signs, wonders, and social miracles to convince people it is of God, Matt. 7:21-23; 2 Thess. 2:9.*
Has a destination – Heaven.	*Has a destination – Hell.*
Presents a relationship with a person, the Lord Jesus Christ, who is able to save a person forever.	*Presents a religion that is powerless to save and will deceive a person into the lake of fire forever. This is Satan's goal!*

If you would like more information on the counterfeit church, you may request a free copy of the author's book, *The Counterfeit Jesus.*

Section 3

WHAT IS GOD'S TRUE CHURCH?

The Disciple's Gospel

By now we should realize that God's idea of the church is not a building where some religious activity is going on.

The word 'church' comes from the Greek word *'ekklesia'* and is translated "church" or "assembly" in the English Bible. In this study, the words church and assembly are synonymous and will be used interchangeably. Our English word *ecclesia*stical, which is commonly associated with church hierarchy, obviously comes from this Greek word.

Definition – *Ekklesia* is composed of two Greek words which mean "called" and "out" or "from" and literally means **ones who are called out from something**. It can refer to something as common as a group of city officials who come apart from the citizens and assemble to discuss city business, Acts 19:39. However, this is the name which God has chosen to call His family of born again children, "called out ones."

One can begin to see why God chose this unique name ('ek' – *out* or *from* and 'kaleo' – *called*) when one studies the calling of believers in the Scriptures. They have been:

- Called *out of* (ek) this world's mind set and system — John 15:19
- Called *out from* (ek) the perishing nations — Acts 15:14
- Delivered *from* (ek) this present evil age — Gal. 1:4
- Delivered *from* (ek) the power of Satan's darkness — Col. 1:13
- Will be physically delivered *out* (ek) of this world into heaven — 2 Cor. 5:8; 1 Cor. 15
- Commanded to come *out of* (ek) the Babylonish system which will experience the fierce wrath of God — Rev. 18:4

People are the Building Stones

We must clearly understand that God's concept of His church is **never, never** a building. Acts 7:48 reveals, *"Howbeit the most High dwelleth not in temples made with hands."* Therefore, it is not a sanctuary made of wood or stones.

However, the true church is human beings who, as guilty sinners before God, were saved out of this world's sin and punishment by repentance and faith in the living Lord Jesus Christ alone. Yes, these people are saved by faith in the One who shed His life's blood as a full payment for their sins. These saved ones are now baptized and indwelt by the Holy Spirit of God Himself and are living to the glory of God. These **people** are now spiritually in union with the Son and therefore are His body. **This is what God recognizes as His true church**.

Living Stones - the True Church

1 Pet. 2:5	"**Ye** [believers] *also, as lively stones, are built up a spiritual house."*
Eph. 1:22,23	*"...the* **church**, *which is his body, the fullness of him that filleth all in all."*
Eph. 2:22	*"In whom* [Christ] **ye** [believers] *also are builded together for an* ***habitation of God*** *through the Spirit."*
1 Cor. 3:16	*"Know ye not that ye* [believers] ***are the temple of God***, *and that the Spirit of God dwelleth in you?"*
1 Cor. 12:13	*"For by one Spirit are we all* [believers] *baptized into one body, whether we be Jews or Gentiles."*
1 Cor. 12:27	*"Now ye* [believers] *are the body of Christ, and members in particular."*

So we have discovered that God's church is not a tangible building, but it is living people super-naturally indwelt by His Holy Spirit. Now, wherever these true Christians meet together to function as an assembly of believers in His Name, they comprise the true church. They may meet in a house such as in Romans 16:5, or a school, or a storeroom, or a mountain cave, or a regular building, but they, rather than the structure, are the building of God.

As one studies the Scriptures he will see that the calling of God's true church in this present world system (which is controlled by the enemy, Satan) may be concisely defined as follows:

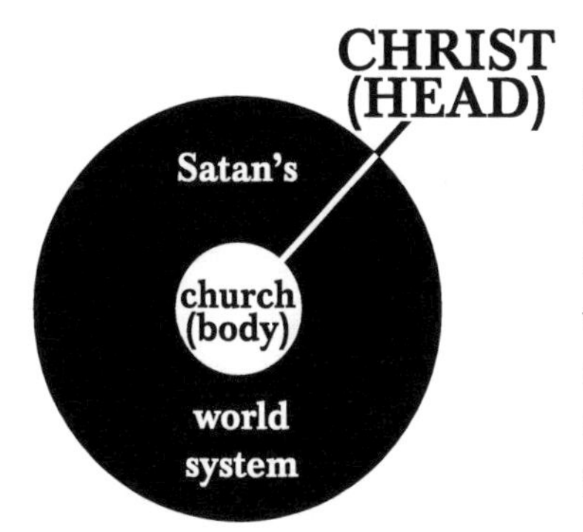

The church is a body of Spirit-born believers who, though in a rebellious world, are sustained and governed by Heaven, the Head – like the Lord Jesus was when on earth. Thus, the church becomes an extension of Christ by its love and subjection to Him, unlike everyone else.

What is the Gospel of the True Church?

> **WARNING** What the Church is not. Above all, we must realize that the church is never the door to heaven. The Savior, the Lord Jesus Christ, is the only door, John 10:9. One must come to Christ alone for salvation and not to the "church." It is not that one becomes saved by going to "church" and doing the various rituals – rather, one becomes a member of God's true church by first being saved, Acts 2:47.

We will note now in our study of the New Testament that the true church's gospel is eternal salvation through Jesus Christ alone and involves 3 stages for the believer. We will call them the "3 Ps" and their order cannot be changed or a false gospel will be created.

Stage #1. Past Action

The believer is "saved" from the **P***enalty of Sin*

In Romans 1 – 5, we see the unbeliever under the **wrath** of God because of his sins, for which he is fully accountable. The price or penalty for those sins is "death," i.e., eternal separation from God in conscious, fiery torment. *"The wages of sin is* ***death****,"* Rom. 6:23. However, Jesus Christ the Lord, by dying for our sins, has taken the penalty for us and paid our debt of sin in full to God. His blood sacrifice is complete and is a once for all-time act of history. Never again does any sacrifice have to be repeated by Christ or by the believer to appease God's wrath.

Thc repentant believer is **instantly** and forever saved from wrath and is not under the condemnation of God. On the action of faith alone in the gospel, the sinner is cleared from his guilty standing and is declared justified (righteous), holy, and reconciled to God. The sinner's law-keeping, church of his choice, rituals, and religious experiences have nothing whatever to do with paying the price of his sin. The penalty is fully paid and God is eternally satisfied. *The victory lies in the Lord Jesus Christ and His* ***death****.*

Stage #2. Present Action

The believer is being "saved" from the **P***ower of Sin*

In Romans 5:12 through chapter 8, we discover that the sinner is not only under the wrath of God, but is also a sinful **wreck** in his character because of his ancestry – a descendant from Adam. That is, he is sold out to sinning, his very Adamic nature refuses to be subject to God. Even after trusting Christ the believer **still** has the powerful law of evil warring in his body which can make him captive to the law of sin.

Therefore, God's salvation is more than just a fire escape. God also deals with the wreckage of sin. Through the gospel, God is delivering the believer from the power of his sinful nature which can devastate his life. He is changing his life to one that is sold out to holiness and good works for the glory of God. God's predestinated plan is *to change the believer into the image of the Son of God.* (As we will see later, this is where the local church plays a major role.)

This stage is not concerned with going to hell or getting into heaven but has everything to do with God's purpose for saving every sinner. Just as one would wash a dirty glass first, with the purpose of then filling it with liquid to serve, so God first cleans us by Christ's blood and then puts ***Christ in us*** so He can use us to serve. Through the holy power of the *"Spirit of life in Christ Jesus,"* He has set us free from the law of sin and death that powerfully dominated our bodies. The Spirit begins a daily process of renewing our thinking and giving us power to do right as we yield to His leading through the Scriptures.

Unlike being saved from wrath, which is instant, being saved from the power of sin (sanctification) is a life-long process. The further good news is that now the resurrected Savior lives as the believer's only high priest; so when a believer sins, upon confession to Jesus, he is totally and immediately cleansed from all impurity by the shed blood of Jesus Christ. Therefore, on the subject of having power to overcome sin, *the victory lies in the resurrected Lord Jesus Christ and His **life** in us through the Spirit.*

Stage #3. Future Action

The believer will be "saved" from the **P***resence of Sin*

In Romans 8:21-23 we discover that, although the believer has the firstfruits of the Spirit, the world is still under the sin curse. This affects our bodies which still groan in deterioration and ultimately decay in death. However, Galatians 1:4 teaches that Jesus *"gave himself for our sins, that he might deliver us from this **present evil world**, according to the will of God and our Father."*

Therefore, there is coming that special day for the believer when the Lord Jesus Christ will descend to the air. He will instantly change our bodies whether dead or alive, and transport us to heaven. We will be saved from the presence of sin in our bodies and also rescued from the presence of this evil world, which will then experience the judgment of an angry God. Yes, our vile body will be changed to be like Christ's glorious body, Phil. 3:21. The mortal will put on immortality and the corruptible body will be clothed in incorruption, 1 Cor. 15. The natural will put on the spiritual and the earthly will wear the heavenly. Praise the Lord, for the day is coming when there will be new heavens and a new earth where **righteousness** will live, 2 Pet. 3:13.

Neither politics, psychology, social reform, medicine, science, positive thinking, nor anything else can deliver the believer from the awful presence of sin, *for the victory lies in the Lord Jesus Christ and His* ***appearing***.

True Salvation

As we have looked at the "3 Ps" of salvation – penalty, power, presence – no wonder Hebrews 2:3 calls it ***"so great salvation."*** No wonder Colossians 3:11 proclaims, ***"Christ is all, and in all."***

These three stages of salvation free a sinner from the wrath of God, from the wreckage of sin, and provide for deliverance from the condemned world. This is what the Bible means by **a saved person**. God's salvation is a complete solution to sin as listed below:

1. Justification – (declared righteous before God) – by faith
2. Sanctification – (being made righteous in life-style) – by the Spirit
3. Glorification – (escaping from the unrighteous world) – by the rapture

This is the gospel and experience of the true church and is given by grace alone. Grace is God giving guilty sinners undeserved, free salvation as a gift of love. As one has so aptly put it, grace is **G**od's **R**iches **A**t **C**hrist's **E**xpense.

So, we have seen that the true church is people who have been called out to a special destination through God's gospel – to be like and with Christ. The church could be likened to a special club for God's children only, for which Jesus Christ paid the dues.

Section 4

Nine Features of the House of God

The Disciple's Home

Just as every house has certain fundamental features, such as a builder, an owner, a foundation, certain materials, and an occupant, so also has the house of God. In the Old Testament one could look at the Jewish temple, God's House, and see gold, pillars, and a holy place. However, in the New Testament, God's house is spiritual instead of physical. As we have learned, God looks at His church as a house, for that is where He lives on earth, *"the **house of God** which is the church of the living God,"* 1 Tim. 3:15. The following are nine dynamic spiritual features of God's present-day house:

#1. Ownership

*"...the church of God, which He...**purchased** with His own blood." Acts 20:28*

The church does not belong to any one group of people for they did not buy it. But the Lord Jesus Christ did. He redeemed the church with His own precious blood. It does not belong to those who follow Martin Luther or to those who happen to practice baptism, etc. Therefore, the church should follow the owner's desires and not the desires of man.

#2. The Builder

*"Upon this rock **I will build** my church." – the Lord Jesus, Matt. 16:18*

It is the Son of God who is the builder of the church. If the church is important enough for Him to be involved in, shouldn't we be also? It is not built by some religious council or by a democratic majority vote of delegates or members but is to be built according to the builder's blueprint – the Word of God. In 1 Corinthians 3, we learn that the Lord Jesus entrusts the building (the outworking of truth) to the ones He has saved. He does this by uniquely gifting every believer, as the Holy Spirit chooses, with certain abilities for the purpose of building up one another. We are responsible, however, to carefully follow the Lord's blueprint.

#3. The Building Materials

"...ye [believers] *as **lively stones** are built up a spiritual house..." 1 Pet. 2:5*

Just as a house is built out of specific materials, so is the church. It is built out of living stones, which are Spirit-born believers. It is not to be built with a mixture of living and dead stones. Although the unsaved can listen and observe the church meetings, they are not to participate in the service or the spiritual activities. In the O.T., an ox (clean animal) and a donkey (unclean) were not to be yoked together when a field was plowed. The fulfillment of this is in 2 Corinthians 6:14-19 where God states that because believers are His temple they are not to be yoked together with unbelievers in spiritual endeavors.

#4. The Occupants

*"...ye are the temple of the living **God;***
as God hath said, **I will dwell in them**.*" 2 Cor. 6:16*

*"**Christ** in you..." Col. 1:27*

"In whom ye also are builded together for an habitation of God
*through the **Spirit**." Eph. 2:22*

Just as a house is designed to have someone living in it, so the church was designed to be the place where God the Father, Son, and Spirit live and operate. The character of the people who live in a house determines what one feels free to bring into it. Since God is holy, we should be very careful not to bring unholy things or bad habits into our lives nor into our local assembly. *"Holiness **becometh** thine house, O Lord, forever,"* Ps. 93:5.

WARNING *1 Cor. 3:17 – "If any man defile the temple of God, him shall God destroy; for the temple of God is holy, which temple ye are."*

#5. The Foundation or Rock

"For other **foundation** *can no man lay than that is laid, which is Jesus Christ." 1 Cor. 3:11*

Just as every house must have a right foundation on which to rest to keep the house a solid unit, so the true church's one foundation and common bond is Jesus Christ the Son of God. Peter calls the Lord Jesus the chief cornerstone, 1 Pet. 2:6.

The church is not to be built on a certain religious creed or tradition but on Jesus Christ Himself – on His deity, His complete blood atonement for sin, His living authority as Lord and only mediator to intercede for sin. A group of people standing on a different foundation are not God's true church but a counterfeit, no matter what name they go by or what else may be right. The foundation must be right or the house will not stand in the day of God's stormy judgment, Matt. 7:24-27.

#6. Headship

"Christ is the head of the church." Eph. 5:23

Just as every house that contains a family should have a head to maintain order, so does the church. We humans tend to want some great leader or organizational headquarters to turn to for direction. We like to follow someone we can see, hear, and touch. But the Lord Jesus is the unseen head, and He wants us by faith to trust and obey Him. Thus, the church should submit to be governed by the Head's Word rather than by some human leader or tradition no matter how great these might be. For Christ has been exalted by God over every level of authority and is *"the head over all things to the church,"* Eph. 1:22.

You see, Satan can corrupt a human headquarters but he cannot corrupt Christ who lives in heaven and is greater than all powers. Praise the Lord! So, why not drink from uncontaminated waters?

A body with no head is dead – a body with more than one head is a monster.

#7. The Name

*"For where two or three are gathered together in **My Name**, there am I in the midst of them." – the Lord Jesus, Matt. 18:20*

Just as one could easily recognize someone's house by the name on the door, so the church should be recognized and known only by Christ's Name. It should never lower itself to adopting the name of a great Christian leader or fly its banner in the name of a great Christian doctrine. Some who would never dream of preaching salvation by any other Name than that of the Lord Jesus Christ (Acts 4:12), do not seem to realize that the Name of the Lord Jesus Christ is also the only Name under heaven God gives the church to gather in and to be known by. Col. 3:17, *"And whatsoever ye do in word or deed,* ***do all in the name of the Lord Jesus****, giving thanks to God and the Father by him."*

> *"It has well been pointed out that in early Christianity there were congregations of believers but no Congregationalists; baptized believers but no Baptists; there were elders or presbyters in the assembly but no Presbyterians; there were methods in their meetings but no Methodists; there were bishops (elders) in the church but no Episcopalians; they trembled at the Word but there were no Quakers; they all shared in the blessings of Pentecost but there were no Pentecostals; they were all united in Christ but there were no United Brethren; they were all brethren in Christ but there were no Plymouth Brethren; they all had charisma (gift of grace) but there were no Charismatics; they all believed in the Messiah but there were no Messianics. The early believers simply met in the Name of the Lord Jesus Christ and so were labeled by the world as Christians."*

#8. The Glory

*"Unto **Him*** [God] *be **glory** in the church by Christ Jesus..." Eph. 3:21*

*"...in all things **He*** [Christ] *might have the preeminence." Col. 1:18*

Just as your house is meant to serve, comfort, and satisfy you, so the house of God is meant for His glory and honor. This is why all adoration and attention should be directed to the Father and the Son, not to entertaining self or glorifying some gifted leader.

That's why such holy titles as "Father," "Reverend," "Holy Father," "Rabbi," "Master" (which is synonymous with teacher or pastor), should be reserved only for the glory of the church, God and Christ. Never should the servant take the master's titles of honor. Notice how your Bible teaches this in Matthew 23:8-12. Also, Psalm 111:9 declares, *"Holy and **reverend*** [awesome] *is* **His** *name."* Not one Christian is ever addressed with these spiritual titles in the Bible. Furthermore, any special religious clothing that distinguishes one group of Christians from another has no place in God's house where Christ is worthy of all the glory.

#9. The Goal

"Looking for that blessed hope [goal], *and the glorious appearing of the great God and our Saviour Jesus Christ." Titus 2:13*

Just as every home has a goal as it raises the children, so does the church. The goal should not be to try to see the world changed into a Christian Utopia through politics or social reform. The day is coming when Christ will return and change it Himself. Our responsibility as ambassadors for Christ (called out ones – church) having a heavenly citizenship, is to be faithful to His Word and to represent Him accurately. As Peter the Apostle exhorted, we are *"strangers and pilgrims"* passing through this world.

To try to Christianize a corrupt world which God has appointed for condemnation is like investing in and remodeling a building which the city has condemned for destruction. We are looking for a better country, i.e., a heavenly one that endures forever, Heb. 11:13-16. May the church stick to its God-given high calling concerning the world: to proclaim the gospel of salvation from God's wrath and of adoption into His family.

We can't improve upon the following statement concerning the church and so we quote:

> **"Instead of the church pursuing her appointed path of separation, persecution, world hatred, poverty and non resistance, she has used Old Testament Scriptures to justify her in lowering her purpose to the civilization of the world, the acquisition of wealth, the use of an imposing ritual, the erection of magnificent church buildings, the invocation of God's blessing upon the conflict of armies and the division of an equal brotherhood into 'clergy' and 'laity'."**

God promises the church that in the last days the world will increase in sin. However, the day is coming when Christ will appear and change it all – ***this is the blessed hope of the church.***

As you studied these 9 features, it should be plain to see that all church teaching is built around the very meaning of the word 'church' – **ones who are called out**. Above all, in God's house *"Christ is all,"* Col 3:11.

So you see, church truth is **Christ-centered** teaching. To look down on God's church is to look down on the Lord Jesus Christ. Ephesians 1:23 defines the church as *"the fullness of **Him**."*

Section 5

The Blueprint for God's Church

The Disciple's Instructions

Some may ask, since the church is not under the law of Israel (their written code to govern their actions), isn't the church to be Spirit-led, to just go by an inner urge and the emotion of the Spirit, as the governing rule for her actions? While the Spirit is dynamically involved, as we shall see later, the answer is *absolutely no*! So is there really a blueprint for the church to follow? The answer is *absolutely yes*! But where do we look for this order and government for God's church? Mainly (and logically), turn to the letters written from God to His believing church. These are the letters from the Apostles of the Lord Jesus Christ – from Romans through Revelation – and they are known as the **Epistles,** letters of instruction.

WARNING To learn church order, do not make the mistake of reading mail addressed to someone else, such as the books to Israel in the Old Testament.

If you were getting a prescription from your doctor to correct a problem, it could be disastrous to pick up your friend's prescription and to follow those instructions. It is not that your friend's prescription wasn't correct for him and true, but it wasn't meant for you.

The New is In - The Old is Out

The New Testament (covenant) is just that – ***new*** – and the old is just that – ***old***. This does not mean that the Old Testament is not God's Word and is not profitable and valuable to read. ***It is!*** As Romans 15:4

and 1 Corinthians 10:11 expound, the O.T. was written so the church could learn by previous examples of patience, hope, character, and the power of God, and could be warned of mistakes to avoid.

There are hundreds of picture-types of the Lord Jesus and His gospel in the O.T., plus scores of dynamic prophecies. One should have a good grip of the Old Testament in order to understand the New Testament more clearly. However, the master design of this new organism called the "body of Christ" was not revealed in the O.T. but kept a *mystery* until Jesus Christ came, Eph. 3:5; 5:32. Remember, a biblical *mystery* is **a plan or truth of God that was kept hidden or secret to past generations, but is now revealed to His chosen ones.** So one will never find the plan of the church explained in the O.T., for it simply was not yet revealed.

To reveal the great plan of the church, God used the apostles, but chiefly Paul. These letters of instruction from the apostles are now part of the New Testament. They were Spirit-inspired letters of encouragement, instruction, rebuke, and correction *written specifically* to the churches or Christians and are called ***'epistles'*.** So this is the "mail" we will read to learn about the church, its calling, order, and government. It's vitally important to realize what testament (covenant) you are living under, so you know what instructions to obey. If you are a believer in the Lord Jesus, *you are the church and the* **epistles** *of the N.T. are your instructions.*

The Book of Acts and the Apostles

The book of the "Acts of the Apostles" records how the risen Lord used His special messengers, called apostles, and gave them unique authority to reveal the plan of the church. Therefore, one must understand that Acts is a transitional book. In it, God is making a stunning change from the God-given law that was 1,480 years old, to a new and living way through His Son Jesus Christ (which was predicted by the law).

Acts is like the foundation of a new house in which you plan to live. There are certain methods and special power machines you use to dig and lay the foundation. However, once you're through, you retire those tools, for the job is done. The rest of the house does not need those special tools and methods. But remember, it is just the tools and methods you put away, not the foundation.

Apostles – Specially Gifted Men to Lay the Foundation

Eph. 2:20 *"And are built upon the* ***foundation*** *of the* ***apostles*** *and prophets, Jesus Christ himself being the chief corner stone."*

Acts 2:43 *"And fear came upon every soul: and many wonders and signs were done* ***by the apostles.****"*

Acts 4:33 *"And with great power gave the* ***apostles*** *witness of the resurrection of the Lord Jesus."*

Acts 19:11 *"And God wrought special miracles by the hands of* ***Paul.****"*

2 Cor. 12:12 *"Truly the* ***signs of an apostle*** *were wrought among you in all patience, in signs, and wonders, and mighty deeds."*

Heb. 2:4 *"God also bearing* ***them*** [apostles] *witness, both with signs and wonders, and with divers miracles, and gifts of the Holy Ghost, according to his own will."*

God used a special breed of men called apostles ("sent messengers") to lay the foundation of the church. To prove they had authority from the resurrected Lord to reveal this new plan, God gave them unique power to do special miracles and signs, such as laying on of hands with tongues following, mass healings in a community, raising the dead, etc. Powerful signs were used by these men to convince the Jews of the transition from old to new and to unite the Gentile believers with the Jewish into one body and church.

As the end of the apostles' mission drew near, and the written epistles of faith and instruction were being circulated among the churches, you will notice a **definite** decrease in these apostolic miracles. Church history also bears this out. No new apostles succeeded them. Their job was finished. The apostles were a special breed of men for a special time with no successors but their word.

Thus, the charter for the church became, not the Mosaic law, but the ***"apostles' doctrine"*** as found in their epistles. In the Scriptures, you will find the church continuing *"steadfastly in the apostles'* ***doctrine****"*, Acts 2:42. You will find that Paul the Apostle directed the believers to his **word** rather than to the Jewish law or to his own experiences as the following scriptures indicate:

Acts 20:32 "*And now, brethren, I commend you to God, and to the word of his grace, which is able to build you up.*"

2 Thess. 2:15 "*Therefore, brethren, stand fast, and hold the traditions which ye have been taught, whether by word, or our epistle.*"

2 Tim. 1:13 "*Hold fast the form of sound words, which thou hast heard of me, in faith and love which is in Christ Jesus.*"

2 Tim. 2:2 "*And the things that thou hast heard of me among many witnesses, the same commit thou to faithful men, who shall be able to teach others also.*"

Yes, the Word of God is now complete and it is the only and final authority. Now the 'epistles', which contain the apostles' doctrine, form the charter for the church, and they are the "apostle" for today – the only authority given by the Lord.

WARNING We must not make the tragic mistake of teaching the experiences of the apostles as the normal Christian life, but rather we must experience the teaching of the apostles.

Never take the book of Acts to fully constitute your doctrine for the church, for it was only the foundation step to the epistles. The experiences of the apostles and early church, including the Jewish transition, are constantly changing in the book of Acts. God is steering the church toward a definite goal, as revealed in the epistles. There are rapid changes in every chapter as the wall of the law is broken down and the body of Christ (church), which is a new creation of both Jewish and Gentile believers, is formed.

The following is a small sampling of the differences in the various experiences in Acts and the **exact order** in which they happened. One should see just how foolish it would be to claim one chapter as the norm for church behavior without the further authority of the epistles.

Acts 2 Jewish Jerusalem	**Acts 8** Hated Samaritan half-breeds	**Acts 10** Italians in Israel	**Acts 19** Jews in Gentile Ephesus
Speakers minus Spirit	Speakers had Spirit	Speakers had Spirit	Water baptized in repentance by John the Baptizer
Sound of rushing wind	Did miracles	No miracles done	Had not heard of the Holy Spirit
Tongues like fire	Converts believed	Heard Word	No miracles
Filled with Spirit	Baptized in water	Believed in Jesus	Heard gospel of Christ
Speakers spoke in tongues	Several days passed with no Spirit	Remission of sins	Water baptized in Jesus' Name
Converts repent	Apostles had to come from Jerusalem	Received Spirit instantly	Paul laid hands on converts
Water baptism	Prayed and laid hands on converts	No laying on of hands	Converts received Holy Spirit
Remission of sins	Converts received Holy Spirit	Converts spoke in tongues	Converts spoke in tongues
Received Holy Spirit	No record of tongues	Water baptism	
No record of converts having tongues			

Always remember that the book of Acts was a bridge as God crossed over from the old to the new:

OLD	ACTS	NEW
The Mosaic Law		The Apostles' Epistles
Works		Grace
The temple		The church
Jews as chosen people		Jews and Gentiles chosen as one body
Old Covenant		New Covenant
The dead letter		A New and Living Way
The altar for lambs		The cross of Jesus
The blood of millions of animals		The blood of Jesus Christ
The bondage of rituals		The life-giving Spirit
A religion you can see		Faith in the unseen, resurrected Savior
Physical blessings		Spiritual blessings
A promised land on earth		A promised position in the heavenlies
613 Ordinances to do or else to die		The Gospel to believe and live forever
Dead Adamic flesh that rebelled		A Spirit-alive person who obeys

So rejoice evermore, Christian. You are in Christ and you are the church!

Here is a chart which should help in understanding the relationship of the church to the Bible and how the epistles are the blueprint-pattern for the church to follow.

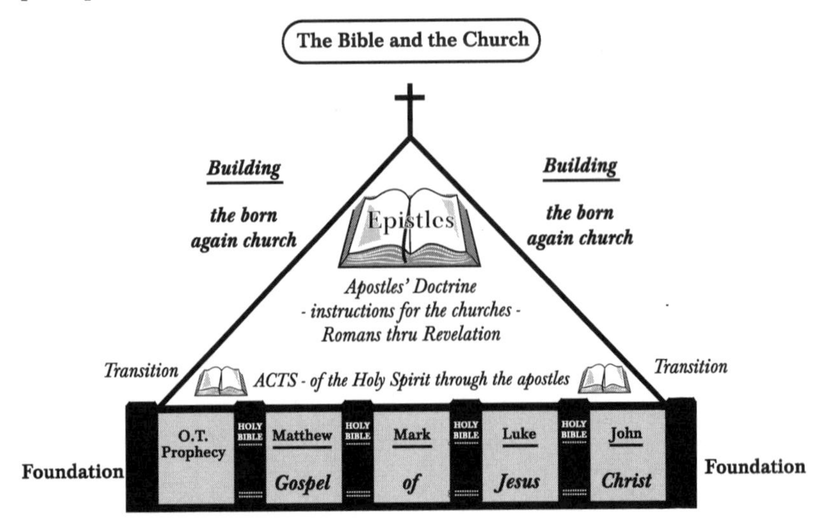

Section 6

The Local Assembly: Its Biblical Basis

The Disciple's Center

We will now consider the clear biblical basis for the local assembly, or church, with which much of the epistles deal.

Definition – ***Local assembly*** – A unit of believers who, with order, habitually meet together in a given area to worship God, to shepherd the sheep, and to teach the Word in order to build up the believers. These believers meet in the Name of the Lord Jesus Christ and under His authority.

One should notice quite readily in the Bible that God talks about *"the church"* and ***"churches."*** *"The Church"* is the body which includes every believer in Christ worldwide (universal), while ***"churches"*** are assemblies of believers in specific localities who form only a small part of the whole body. The New Testament uses specific terminology so one can see whether the verse is talking about the universal church (all believers) or just the local assembly church (a group of believers). For example:

1. *"all the* ***churches****"* – 1 Cor. 14:33	**Many local churches**
2. *"the* ***church of God*** *which is at Corinth"* – 1 Cor. 1:2	**The local church in one specific city**
3. *"unto the* ***churches*** *of Galatia"* – Gal. 1:2	**Different local churches in a state or region**
4. *"His body's sake which is the* ***church****"* – Col. 1:24	***Every believer*** **in the world**

As has been said before, to become a member of the body of Christ (the universal church), one must simply receive by faith Jesus Christ as Savior and Lord, Gal. 3:26. However, the local assembly of believers involves more than faith. The local assembly has an order and government so it can function for its God-given purpose. There is only one body but there are many expressions of it through the local assemblies.

> **Example** – All McDonald's employees are members of the McDonald's Corporation. Whatever benefits and securities go with being a part of McDonald's are theirs. But the McDonald's Corporation consists of thousands of local units in many cities throughout the world. Each unit will have certain trademarks in common with all the others since they are all part of one corporation. But each unit will also consist of managers, a structure, and regulations to reach its goal. Thus, an employee who wants to progress will have to put himself under the authority of his local unit and be a working part of it. So it is with the believer and the church.

Notice the Differences

You will notice in the New Testament that sometimes God uses the phrase "in Christ" and sometimes the phrase "in the church." "In Christ" is speaking of the believer's position and benefits in the Savior, while "in the church" is speaking of the believer's conduct in a local assembly. There is a great difference between the two and it needs to be correctly understood today to avoid error.

In the following chart is a list of 7 major differences between the universal church, which includes every believer, and the local church, which is an assembly of believers.

The Universal Church Foundational Truth – "in Christ"	***The Local Church*** *Building Truth – "in Christ"*
#1. No Differences – All believers are one in Christ and all share the same standing with God no matter what their nationality, gender, or social class, Gal. 3:26,28.	***Differences in Authority*** – *Some have the rule or leadership over others in an orderly way, Heb. 13:17; 1 Thess. 5:12.*
#2. No Distinctions – Male and female are one in Christ and both are equally saved by faith alone. Both are joint heirs of Abraham and eternal life, Gal. 3:28,29.	***Distinctions in Roles*** – *There are definite differences of roles for the man and woman in God's local assembly, 1 Cor. 14:34; 1 Tim 2:8-12.*
#3. Security – One can never be put out of the body of Christ, John 10:27,28; Eph. 4:30.	***Not Secure*** – *One can be put away (excommunicated) for a time. There is an outside and an inside, 1 Cor. 5:13; 2 Thess. 3.*
#4. Only God – The Lord, not man, adds one to the body. No man can save you, but Christ alone, Acts 2:47; 1 Cor. 12:13.	***Man Involved*** – *The local brethren are to receive one into the fellowship, care, and authority of a church – in the Lord, Rom. 16:1,2; Acts 18:27.*
#5. No Ordinances – To be saved and in the body requires faith plus nothing! "Not by works," Col. 2:14; Rom. 3:28.	***Ordinances*** – *There are ordinances such as baptism, the Lord's Supper, head-covering, etc., 1 Cor. 11, 14; Acts 2:41,42.*
#6. Position the Same – The position by grace alone, for every believer in Christ is equally forgiven, holy, and blameless before God in love, Eph. 1.	***Performance Different*** – *The performance of believers and churches is not always equal and is not always holy and without blame, Rev. 2, 3.*
#7. One Body – All believers are viewed as just one body in Christ, with every believer being equally a priest through the blood of Christ, 1 Pet. 2:5,9; 1 Cor. 12:13.	***Many Members*** – *Each individual believer is looked upon as a unique member of the local body, with different gifts and functions to give and use. However, all should be working together as one, Rom. 12; 1 Cor. 12.*

The **7** differences are designed to show that the local church is a distinct entity with a definite order for it, as clearly taught in the Bible. The differences exist because the purpose of Christ and the purpose for His church are different. Christ the Lord's purpose was to lay down His life as a blood sacrifice to give the gift of everlasting life to all who believe. The purpose of the church is not to re-do this, but to be a witness of His sacrifice and Lordship by its word and life.

While being part of the universal church is not based on the believer's spiritual condition, the local church is concerned about a believer's spiritual condition. For the local church is to be a testimony to the Lord Jesus Christ by its love and subjection to the most high God.

After considering the preceding truth, it should be evident that a local church is more than just a few believers meeting together for fellowship over coffee or for a Bible study.

Keep in mind that the truths of the universal church come first. These are fundamental, and every true local church must have her roots in these truths and must grow from this living foundation, which is Christ Jesus the Lord.

WARNING The two aspects of the church universal and local are different, **yet not to be separated**. The one rests on the other. The local church is built on the foundation of the universal church – Christ and His work for every believer, Eph. 2:20-22; 4:1-16. To fail to see this is to open the door to sectarianism and legalism.

Section 7

The Purpose of the Local Assembly

The Disciple's Goals

Since the church can neither forgive one's sin nor take one to heaven, we ask then, why did God form churches on earth? To be witnesses to Him, to be sure. But being a witness to others of the gospel would surely not require all the details connected with a church. So we ask again, what is the real reason for an assembly of believers to meet together as an orderly local church?

The Lord Jesus revealed part of the purpose in John 4:23, *"But the hour cometh, and now is, when the true worshippers shall worship the Father in spirit and in truth: for the Father seeketh such* ***to worship him.****"* In an enemy world controlled by Satan, a world which is anti-God, anti-Christ, anti-holiness, and anti-truth, the Father delights in a minority who will give Him the worth and honor He is due. As we shall see in more detail a little later in this study, the local assembly of believers is meant to worship and glorify God.

But in order to witness **correctly** for God and to worship Him in **truth,** we find we need this first and primary purpose of a church meeting. **The church meeting is created by God for the believer's edification.** Believers need to be built up and to be made strong in their faith. Just because one is saved does not mean he is mature with full knowledge of God and able to serve Him effectively. This is where the local church comes into the picture.

> **Example** – As a car battery needs to be recharged, or a body needs rest and proper nutrition to function properly, so the Christian needs to be built up spiritually. As a car can't go far without a stop at the gas pumps for energy, so

a Christian can't worship and serve God effectively and satisfactorily without God's assembly church.

God's purpose for the church meeting as revealed in 1 Corinthians 14 is:

"He that prophesieth ***edifieth*** [builds up] *the church."* (v.4)
"That the church may receive ***edifying.****"* (v.5)
"Seek that ye may excel to the ***edifying*** *of the church."* (v.12)
"Let all things be done unto ***edifying.****"* (v.26)
"That all may learn, and all may be ***comforted.****"* (v.31)

Ephesians 4:12 clearly teaches the **3** main reasons God has given a variety of gifted men to the church.

#1. "For the perfecting of the saints" – So the believer can become mature and Christ-like in character. Thus, the church is a place to be fed the Word so one can grow.

#2. "For the work of the ministry" – The purpose of being fed properly and growing strong is so the believer can also be involved in the work of serving God.

#3. "For the edifying of the body of Christ" – The purpose of serving God is so the built up believer can now, with his gifts and maturity, build up other believers. The cycle continues. Thus, the grand goal is reached of all believers not remaining babies and children but growing into *"the stature* [complete likeness] *of the fullness of Christ."* God will then be magnified.

WARNING Although one can read on his own and listen to tapes, it is when the church meets together that the Lord Jesus promised to be in the midst, Matt. 18:20. Therefore, in a unique way the Spirit, by using a variety of believers when assembled together, will freshly minister to the current needs of His sheep. Forsaking the assembling together of the church **robs one** of this blessing of the Lord which one needs for effective growth.

The overseers (elders) of a local assembly are exhorted to *"feed the church of God,"* Acts 20:28, for it is the *"word of His grace which is able to build you up,"* 20:32. The food that the church is to receive is not drama, entertainment, psychology, political propaganda, or the traditions of men, but the Word of God. God claims the holy Scriptures will not only make one wise unto salvation, but will completely equip a believer to every good work. Quite a claim!

God claims in 2 Timothy 3:16 that the Scriptures are profitable for:

"Doctrine"	–	what is right
"Reproof"	–	what is not right
"Correction"	–	how to get right
"Instruction"	–	how to keep right.

Sad and weak will be the church that neglects one of the primary reasons for meeting together – *the consistent teaching of the all sufficient living Word.*

The Four Main Activities of the Assembly

Acts 2:42 and the epistles reveal to us the four activities of the church meeting.

1. Doctrine	The preaching of the Word
2. Fellowship	Getting to know, love, help, and learn from each other
3. Breaking of Bread	Remembering (worshiping) the Lord by taking of the Lord's Supper
4. Prayers	Thanking and laying hold of God for guidance and power

These four activities of the assembly are its reason for existing. This is God's table, i.e., His provision for His children. Don't take just part of the menu, but take all four, or you will be spiritually malnourished. This is why we meet together. This is why the Lord repeatedly says, "come together."

Never forget, the assembly is designed for the believer and for God's glory, rather than for the unbeliever and his need.

Understanding this vital truth will greatly affect your attitude toward the church.

> **WARNING** Never compromise God's truth to make the assembly meeting appealing to the unsaved. It was never designed for the unsaved, nor to be appealing to them. It was created so the church would be built up and then would reach out with the saving gospel which was designed for the unbeliever.

The Six Metaphors of the Church

Following are six metaphors or symbols which God uses to describe His church. They are: **1.** House, **2.** Lampstand, **3.** Body, **4.** Temple, **5.** Vineyard (garden), and **6.** Engaged Virgin (bride). These symbols are used by God to help us further understand the calling and purpose of the church. Let's now look at each one more closely.

#1. A House

"The house of God, which is the church of the living God, the pillar and ground of the truth." 1 Tim. 3:15

Just as a house needs to be cleaned often, so also does the church.

The metaphor of a house relates to us the fact that God lives in the church. Therefore, just as a good housekeeper keeps her house free from dirt and germs for the occupants, so the church must be kept free from sin for God's sake. Since the God of truth and holiness lives in this house and the world associates His Name with the church, pure truth must be upheld for all to see, and holiness must be maintained at all cost. 1 Peter 1:16 states: *"Be ye **holy;** for I am holy."* Again, Peter speaks in chapter 4 verse 17: *"...that judgment must begin at the **house of God.**"* Psalm 93:5 also states: *"**Holiness** becometh thine **house**, O Lord, forever."*

#2. A Lampstand

"The seven candlesticks [lampstands] *which thou sawest are the seven churches." Rev. 1:20*

As a light overcomes darkness, so also does the church.

This metaphor teaches us that just as a light does away with darkness and shows what is reality, the church's mission is to shine in a dark world of sin by being a witness and testimony of the One who said: *"I am the light of the world,"* John 8:12.

Though the world is blinded by Satan to the glorious light of Jesus Christ, the church can shine forth in the darkness for *"God, who commanded the light to shine out of darkness, **hath shined in our hearts,*** **to give the light** *of the knowledge of the glory of God in the face of Jesus Christ,"* 2 Cor. 4:6.

The church is looked at as a lighthouse in a dark and stormy world. *"That ye may be blameless and harmless, the sons of God, without rebuke, **in the midst of a crooked and perverse nation**, among whom ye shine as lights in the world; holding forth the word of life,"* Phil. 2:15,16.

The church shines forth by its blameless life, which adds real power to its proclamation of the "Word of Life." Remember, if the lens of a flashlight is dirty, the light will not shine clearly. So if our life is dirty (sinful), the world won't see the light of Christ shining through us.

#3. A Body

"...the church, which is His body..." Eph. 1:22,23

As a body needs to exercise
to keep in shape,
so does the church.

As one uses his body to serve himself, so God uses His church to serve Himself. The church is the Lord's hands, feet, and mouth. ***This is a dynamic truth!***

Body truth also teaches the believer that no man is an island unto himself. Just as each member of our body needs the others, so, serving the Lord through the framework of the church keeps us dependent and responsible to others (a check and balance system). This was designed by God to discourage independence and to reduce the risk of erroneous teaching.

WARNING Even a Christian organization or outreach campaign or magazine, can slip into the dangerous trap of becoming a separate section of the one body, thus operating independently of God's designed government and commands through the local church. This could lead to unscriptural methods used in serving God and cause believers to rally around an organization instead of around the Lord and His assembly.

The truth of "one body" also introduces us to the truth of only **one Head** – the Lord Jesus Christ. The head supplies the brains, the power, and the guidance that the body needs. The local church has no visible head or headquarters on earth – only the unseen Head, Christ, who is in heaven. Remember, a body with more than one head is a monster.

Body truth also introduces us to the only membership God knows about. Scripture never teaches that a believer is a "member" of a local church with its name and style as our exclusive banner to fly. A believer is looked at as being a "member" of the body of **Christ** only.

#4. A Temple

"Unto the church of God which is at Corinth
...Know ye not that ye are the temple of God." 1 Cor. 1:2; 3:16

As a temple was designed for offering to God, so is the church.

The word temple takes us back to the O.T. and is associated with the giving of **worship** to the one true God through the priesthood. 1 Peter 2:5 tells the believer that he is a holy priest in God's house (temple) in order to *"**offer up** spiritual sacrifices, acceptable to God by Jesus Christ."*

When one came to the temple, it was not always to bring a sin sacrifice. Sometimes a burnt offering or the offering of firstfruits was given to God in worship. Deuteronomy 26:10 teaches: *"And now, behold, **I have brought the firstfruits of the land**, which thou, O LORD, hast given me. And thou shalt set it before the LORD thy God, and **worship*** *before the LORD thy God."* Numbers 18:12 shows that the offering to God by the worshipers was to be the best, not what was leftover; *"All the **best** of the oil, and all the **best** of the wine, and of the wheat, the **firstfruits** of them which they shall offer **unto the LORD**, them have I given thee."*

So when we look at the church through the metaphor of a temple, it reminds us to give our best to God. And we are not only to give our money, but also our lives as a living sacrifice, which includes our praises (the fruit of our lips) to the One who is worth it, Heb. 13:15. Are you coming to God's church to offer, or just to receive a blessing for your**self**?

#5. A Garden

"...ye are God's husbandry [vineyard or garden]." 1 Cor. 3:9

As a garden or vine needs to be pruned to produce much fruit, so does the church.

The metaphor of a garden conveys the idea of bearing fruit for the owner of the garden to enjoy and use. Christians are to bring forth the fruit of the Spirit, which is the life of Christ. To produce this fruit God often prunes, bringing trials into our life to draw us closer to Him. As a garden yields fruit, sweet fragrances, and beauty to the owner, so also should the church to God. Paul the apostle spoke of a Christ-centered life as being a sweet aroma unto God, *"For we are unto God a sweet savour* [aroma] *of Christ,"* 2 Cor. 2:15.

However, it is good to remember that in God's garden some are just at the "blade" stage, others are at the "ear" stage, and still others are at the "full corn in the ear" stage, Mark 4:28. Matthew 13:8 speaks of thirty-fold fruit-bearing, sixty-fold fruit-bearing, and hundred-fold fruit-bearing. John 15 puts it this way: "fruit" – "more fruit" – and "much fruit." *Notice, though, that all stages have both life and fruit.*

#6. An Engaged Virgin (Bride)

"For I have espoused [engaged] *you to one husband, that I may present you as a chaste virgin to Christ."* 2 Cor. 11:2

As a bride's love

is expressed by purity,

so is

the church's.

This metaphor teaches us purity in the relationship between Christ and His church. 2 Corinthians 7:1 tells the church: *"Dearly beloved, let us cleanse ourselves from all filthiness of the flesh and spirit* [moral and religious error]." Just as a husband would not want his wife running around and giving her affection to other men, so the Lord Jesus wants His bride (the church) to keep her affection and time for only Him. He does not want the church to play the whore and to lose her virginity by yielding to false gospels or the pleasures of this world system.

Being the bride of Christ vividly pictures the deep love relationship and closeness between Christ and His church. The bridegroom cherishes His bride. He pours all His love and blessings on her.

The bride responds by receiving, loving, submitting, and obeying her bridegroom.

We have seen that God's purpose in the local church is primarily to bring His children to close fellowship with Himself and thus to maturity.

Section 8

THE POWER OF AN ASSEMBLY

The Disciple's Source

The church was birthed in an age of rank paganism, Pharisaic legalism, and anti-Christ Judaism. The church did not possess the resources needed to succeed, as it had neither monetary, military, political, nor religious clout. The infant church was but a small gathering of disciples, most of whom were uneducated; their only training was that they had been with Jesus. Yet within a few short years, without any modern means of transportation and communication, thousands were saved and scores of local churches were established in various parts of the world.

Paul the apostle, in only about a six-year period involving two missionary trips and thousands of miles, saw local assemblies for Christ established in four major provinces of the Roman Empire. These were in Galatia (Turkey), Achaia (Greece), Macedonia (Europe), and Asia Minor (part of Turkey). Quite an achievement even by today's standards!

We therefore ask the question, where did the **power** come from to effect this massive growth of the church? Basically one entity, **the Holy Spirit!** *"But ye shall receive **power**, after that the Holy Ghost is come upon you,"* Acts 1:8. The risen Lord, through the same Spirit who created the world and who raised Him from the dead, miraculously built His church by a variety of gifts and means, against all human odds

While not trying to match the statistics or to use the methods God used with the early church and thus put God in a box, there are 3 main areas of the Holy Spirit's work that were the power then and still are the true power for any believer or local assembly. They are: **prayer** in the Spirit, **preaching** the Word of the Spirit, and

purity in the life of a Spirit-filled believer.

1. Prayer

The early church was a praying church. They prayed in the power of the Holy Spirit and showed their complete dependence on God and God alone for power. Acts 4:31, *"And when they had* ***prayed****, the place was shaken where they were assembled together; and they were all filled with the Holy Ghost, and they spake the word of God with boldness."* In the church's battle against the devil and his powers, we are exhorted to be *"****praying always*** *with all prayer and supplication in the Spirit,"* Eph. 6:18.

Prayer in the energy of the Spirit is simple, but it is also hard work. There is no glory to self. It is the only link to God's power. In spite of this, many local churches have a hard time getting Christians to come together to pray.

2. Preaching the Word

Through the apostles the early church did not offer philosophy, psychology, or political theories in order to change the world. They preached the pure Word of God, the holy Scriptures. We are told that *"they that were scattered abroad went every where preaching the word,"* Acts 8:4, and that the early assembly *"spake the word of God with boldness,"* Acts 4:31. They knew that the power to change lives lay not in their theories, but in the Spirit-inspired Word. *"For the word of God is quick* [life-giving], *and powerful, and sharper than any two-edged sword,"* Heb. 4:12. *"The sword of the Spirit, which is the word of God,"* Eph. 6:17. *"The word of his grace, which is able to build you up,"* Acts 20:32.

May God help the church today to realize that her power is only in the Spirit-gifted preaching of the pure Word in its proper context (rightly divided), and therefore to stick to the Word and only the Word.

3. Purity in the Life

Paul, the apostle, reveals the power that caused a great awakening and resulted in an assembly being planted in Thessalonica as he states, *"For our gospel came* ***not*** *unto you* ***in word only****, but also in* ***power****,* ***and in the Holy Ghost****, and in much assurance;* [how did it?] *as ye know what manner of men we were among you for your sake...how holily and justly and unblameably we behaved ourselves among you that believe,"* 1 Thess. 1:5; 2:10. Yes, holy lives (not living in sin) give full power to prayer and the Word.

Since it is the Holy Spirit who is the church's power, we must be aware of the one thing that grieves (short circuits) the power of the Spirit. Ephesians 4 teaches that **sin** is what grieves *"the Holy Spirit of God."* This is illustrated for us in First Corinthians. The Corinthian church had written to Paul for advice on money matters, marriage, spiritual gifts, and the eating of meats. However, before Paul ever dealt with any of those issues (chapters 7-16), he addressed a problem in the church that they hadn't mentioned – **the sin of fighting and division in the assembly and the sin of immorality** (chapters 1-6). He commanded that sin must first be dealt with and judged in the church.

Another vivid lesson on how sin will cause an assembly to lose power is found in Joshua 8. The children of Israel were able to defeat their enemies against incredible odds by the power of Jehovah. But because one man had sinned, when they came up against the weak city of Ai, they were soundly defeated. The power of the Lord had left them because of sin. The power did not return until that sin was put away.

Many Christians today blame the weakness of the church on everything from the preachers to the program. It might very well be that sinful and worldly lives are the problem.

> A revival is needed from God in each church that has lowered itself to become an entertainment center, or a social club, or "non offensive" to keep the numbers high. Instead of prayer, preaching, and purity being given the primary place, many churches attempt to grow by the pseudo powers of **money**, **methods,** and **modern education**. That is, they collect much money and have beautiful buildings and entertaining Christian programs. They use all kinds of methods based on corporate business strategy to succeed, such as using only the trained professional and highly educated person to teach the flock. Sometimes the numbers of "members" may be high, but where is the power of quality, holy, and biblical living that brings God glory?

God's way is through the power of the Holy Spirit by prayer, preaching, and purity. Simple? **Yes**. Involves the wisdom of man? **No**. This has always been God's "formula" for success. It worked in the early church and it still works now.

A Spirit-filled life that is living in purity +

laying hold of God in fervent and continuing prayer for open doors and hearts +

preaching the Word with boldness =

true spiritual blessing as God works through you.

May each local assembly never lose sight of her true power.

Section 9

The Authority of the Church

The Disciple's Submission

A. The Authority to Judge

A common expression among many groups is, "the Bible says not to judge." This expression is often used to try to defend some unbiblical action. The expression "judge not" becomes a "carte blanche" to justify whatever one feels is right with no reference to biblical absolutes as guides to what is right or wrong in God's eyes.

Meet Authority and Accountability

God has clearly ordained authority and accountability in His church. No corporation in the world attempts to run its organization without management to enforce authority and without demanding accountability to promote correct action. In Matthew chapters 16 and 18 and 1 Corinthians 5 and 6, the church of Jesus Christ is given God-ordained authority to bind and to loose. This authority does not involve judging the unsaved world (*"them that are without God judgeth"*), but it does involve judging the saved (*"judge them that are within"*).

Warning This authority does not authorize the church to create new teachings or traditions and then to bind them upon the "members," as some false churches teach. The church is to stay within the bounds of the Bible.

As you read the context of these passages, you will discover that the authority of the church (through its proper eldership) covers three main areas.

1. **Divisions** – to resolve personal disputes between believers.
2. **Morals** – to discipline sin in unrepentant believers.
3. **Doctrine** – to keep the church doctrinally pure.

The Lord Jesus taught that when believers can't settle their own problems they are to *"TELL IT UNTO THE CHURCH."* There are 4 points to keep in mind that Matthew 18:15-20 teaches on this subject as the church reaches its final verdict on the problem.

1. Christ Himself will be in the midst of the praying church to give it wisdom to help solve the problem.
2. The church's final verdict and decision is binding. It must be obeyed by the believers.
3. Heaven itself sanctions and agrees with the judgment.
4. There is no higher court of appeal. The church is the highest court on earth for Christians.

Authority promotes order and holiness because it brings the disciples into a place of accountability for their actions. Sometimes people become wayward after they have been saved by grace because, they reason, they cannot be judged in hell for their sins. However, having shepherds in an assembly who understand that an assembly has authority to scripturally discipline a believer tends to put a fear of sin in the believer because he realizes there is some consequence for his sin after all. *"Them that sin rebuke before all, that others also may fear,"* 1 Tim. 5:20.

To Judge or Not to Judge?

As we study the Word of God, we begin to see that the philosophy of a Christian "never judging" is a myth, a lie. It would be impossible for an assembly to fulfill its Christ-given authority if it couldn't judge. It would be impossible even to live a safe and healthy life without judging. For who doesn't make judgment decisions concerning medicine, good or bad food, the right partner for life, the best value for your money, etc.? What government exists that doesn't have law and order and that judges its offenders? Who would want to live in a city without policemen? So, let's not be surprised that God authorizes his children to judge good and evil.

True, the Bible says "judge not," but let us read the rest of the verse in John 7:24. *"Judge not according to the appearance, but* ***judge*** *righteous judgment."* Thus, we see the Lord Jesus is telling Christians **to** judge. The caution is that when judging a situation as good or evil, it is necessary to get all the facts and not just to judge by outward evidence alone.

Definition – The word "judge" in the Greek is either *anakrino* or *krino. Anakrino* means to discern, examine, question, and scrutinize. *Krino* means to pick out, select, conclude, decide, choose, approve, or disapprove. Again, these are activities that we do in our everyday life – how much more ought we to judge in things relating to a Holy God?

There are 4 areas the Bible commands the Christian not to judge and 4 areas the Bible commands the Christian to judge. They are as follows.

Four Areas We **ARE NOT** to Judge

1 **HEART MOTIVES** – *"But with me it is a very small thing that I should be judged of you, or of man's judgment...* ***Therefore judge nothing*** *before the time, until the Lord come, who both will bring to light the hidden things of darkness, and will make manifest* ***the counsels of the hearts:*** *and then shall every man have praise of God,"* 1 Cor. 4:3,5.

We are not to judge a person's motives. That is, we must not jump to conclusions about why a person did something. Since we cannot read hearts, we should not accuse a fellow Christian of wrong motives such as self-glory or power-hunger or money-grasping, though their actions may seem to point that direction.

2 **Outward Appearance** – *"**Judge not** according to the appearance...Look not on his countenance...for the LORD seeth not as man seeth; for man looketh on the **outward appearance**, but the LORD looketh on the heart,"* John 7:24; 1 Sam. 16:7.

We must never judge a book by its cover or by how a thing appears to our eyes. We must be careful to get the facts and then to compare the situation with the Word of God.

3 **Another's Liberty** – *"For one believeth that he may eat all things: another, who is weak, eateth herbs...Let us **not therefore judge** one another any more,"* Rom. 14:2,13.

The New Covenant clearly teaches that the Jewish law, with its ceremonies, ordinances, and customs, stood only until the time of reformation (Christ) and it is nailed to His cross. Thus, we are freed and liberated from the bondage of the law. However, there are some Christians who, on an individual basis due to their culture and weak understanding of the new liberty in Christ Jesus, will continue to do things the Bible doesn't command anymore. Thus, we have some Christians who are convicted that a thing is wrong for them in a certain area and other Christians convicted it is right for them in this same area. Rather than judge each other as unspiritual, we should receive one another in the faith of Christ Jesus, which we both have in common.

4 **Another's Actions When You are Doing the Same Thing** – *"**Judge not**, that ye be not judged...And why beholdest thou the mote that is in thy brother's eye, **but considerest not the beam** that is in thine own eye?"* Matt. 7:1,3.

Although, as we will see, the church is allowed to judge a fellow believer's actions when he is wrong, that privilege is lost when the one judging is guilty of a similar action himself. One becomes a hypocrite and a powerless judge when he points out the splinter in his brother's eye without first removing the board in his own eye. However, once the board (wrong) is removed from his own eye, then the Lord says he could and should remove the splinter (fault) from his brother's eye.

Four Areas We **ARE** to Judge

1 **Ourselves** – *"For if we would* ***judge ourselves****, we should not be judged,"* 1 Cor. 11:31.

The Bible is very clear that we should be constantly judging what is right and wrong in our own lives. This way we can save being chastened by the Lord. We do not give an account of our brother to God, but every Christian will give an account of himself, Rom. 14:13.

2 **Actions that are Good or Bad** – *"...in all judgment, that ye may approve things that are excellent,"* Phil. 1:9,10.

The Bible is also clear that there are "absolutes" in the eyes of God, and we are to call sin "sin" and good "good." It is not really we who are judging the action as right or wrong, but God through His Word. This type of judging is simply agreeing with the Judge of all the earth, God.

3 **Doctrine** – *"Let the prophets speak two or three, and let the other judge...Despise not prophesyings. Prove* [test or judge] *all things; hold fast that which is good,"* 1 Cor. 14:29; 1 Thess. 5:20,21.

Just as we are very careful what kind of physical food we eat, so also we should be careful about our spiritual diet. Since Satan is alive, and false or erring teaching abounds which can overthrow one's faith, we are commanded to judge teaching as being good or bad. Again, the standard of comparison is not our own opinion or church tradition but the infallible Word of God.

4 **Sin in the Church** – *"Do not ye judge them that are within* [the assembly]*?...Therefore put away* [excommunicate] *from among yourselves that wicked person,"* 1 Cor. 5:12,13.

The local assembly, through its proper eldership, has authority from the Lord Jesus Christ to judge sin that may occur in a fellow believer's life. These serious sins, that bring shame to the testimony of Jesus Christ, are carefully listed in the Bible and are not left to our imagination. More will be said on this subject in section 9, part B.

We have seen from the Bible that the myth of never judging is unbiblical. When the church makes a judgment concerning a personal dispute or sin in a believer's life, heaven itself agrees with that judgment, and God will hold the person responsible for his reaction to that judgment, Matt. 18.

May God help the modern church to repent and to take up its God given authority. Instead of being spineless and worldly, we must purge sin out of the church of the living God. Instead of taking refuge in "being loving like Christ" as an excuse for not bringing believers into accountability for their deeds of sin and doctrine, we must face God's definition of love: "[love] *rejoiceth not in iniquity, but rejoiceth in the truth,"* 1 Cor. 13:6. As 1 Peter 4:17 states:

> *"For the time is come that* ***judgment*** *must begin at the house of God."*

B. Church Discipline and Boundary Lines

This is an age when freedom, liberty, and personal "rights" are key issues. People desire liberty, some even going to the extreme of "do your own thing." This philosophy isn't new, for thousands of years ago when the children of Israel had departed from God, their style was *"every man did that which was right in his own eyes,"* Judg. 21:25.

WARNING In an age when everyone is concerned about "human rights," God, as Creator, as Savior, and as our Lord, has "owner rights" over us. Let's not forget the rights of God. *"Know ye not that ye are not your own? For ye are bought with a price,"* 1 Cor. 6:19,20.

Often when new believers are saved from the rules, rituals, and false doctrine of religion, they are ecstatic over their new liberty in Christ Jesus alone. Since all the pressure for salvation is gone and their sins are completely forgiven through the blood of Jesus Christ alone, they are rejoicing in the fact that Christ has made them free, John 8:32,36. And they should be encouraged to stand fast in the liberty wherewith Christ has made them free from religious error and the bondage of legalism, Gal. 5:1. This is right and good.

However, when they are introduced to God's local church with its outward testimony, its government, and its God-controlled order, they tend to become puzzled about what might look like a return to legalism. But we must not forget that although the church is not for the saving of the soul, it is to be a witness for Christ Jesus by its **life** and **word**. This is where true Christianity differs from organized religion.

So then, being a lighthouse to the world, the church does have a very definite governmental role in order to fulfill its calling. **Yet, within this governmental order there is much liberty to operate.** If a local assembly, however, adds rules and regulations which cannot be found in Scripture and **binds** them upon the believers, then that is legalism. But if these regulations are found in the Bible in their correct context, then obedience is called for and this is godliness.

In an age which is confused on this issue, may the following Scriptural definition of legalism help:

What Legalism is

- When either the Jewish law or the traditions of men are presented as something which will help earn one's salvation.

- When parts of the Jewish law or the traditions of men are bound upon believers as a **must** for their lifestyle (rather than a personal preference).
- When believers are looked at as less spiritual if they don't conform to these outward rules. (See the book of Galatians, Romans 14, and Colossians 2 for this truth.)

What Legalism isn't

- When a command of the New Testament is taught to the church, not as a means of being saved, but as a means of **pleasing** God. Obedience to His Word is never, never legalism, but rather it is love. (See Titus 2, Romans 6, John 14:15-24, and 1 Corinthians 14:37.)

Boundary Lines

As we proceed, we must realize that the local assembly has boundary lines or limits. Consider in general how that the absence of boundary lines results in chaos and confusion. The United States was formed with much valued freedom of speech. Yet that does not give one the right and freedom to falsely cry "fire" in a public place. A hawk is free as it flies into the blue, but it too has God given boundary lines of atmosphere, gravity, water, to name a few.

These boundary lines are there so we can enjoy our freedom to the max, for without bounds there is the potential for great disaster. We couldn't live without boundary lines. A super highway has boundary lines so the thousands of cars will maintain order and safety. A jetliner that's landing would be wise to stay within the boundary lines of the runway. We wouldn't encourage the pilot in the name of freedom to go beyond them. Also, every game in the sports world is performed within certain boundary lines – again to maintain order and control. So, let's not be surprised that our loving God and all-wise Father has set boundary lines for His church. Do you know where God draws the line?

Out of Bounds

Wherever there are boundary lines, there is automatically an inside and an outside. Thus, God's local assembly is to have an

inside and an **outside** to it. In 1 Corinthians 5 we read that the assembly has a ***"within"*** and a ***"without."*** This brings us to that key truth called SEPARATION.

There are two main areas from which the church is to separate, areas where God has clearly drawn the line. These two areas are out of bounds for God's church. #1. **The world** with its sin, ungodly entertainment, and humanistic philosophy. #2. **False religion and doctrine** with its anti-biblical teaching. Before we examine these two areas and the penalty (discipline) the church gives for a believer who goes out of bounds, let us look at the chart below which illustrates the church of God and its boundary lines.

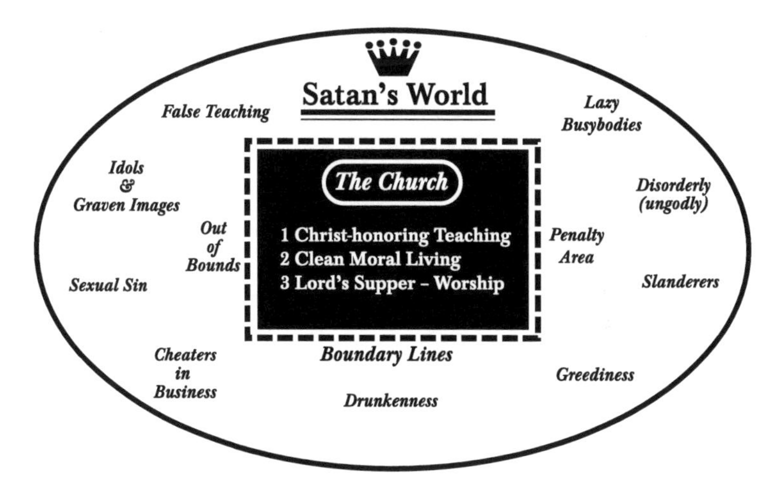

#1. Separation from the World

"And be not conformed to this world." Rom. 12:2
"Know ye not that the friendship of the world is enmity with God?" James 4:4

The church is to be separate from the world system, for the world is controlled by Satan and is in rebellion against God. A believer will hurt himself and lose eternal reward by stepping out of bounds into the world's sin and lifestyle. Titus 2:12 states, *"Teaching us that, denying ungodliness and worldly lusts, we should live soberly, righteously, and godly, in this **present world.**"*

The Penalty for Going Out of Bounds

A) The Charge – The local church has God-given authority to penalize (discipline) the professing believer who steps out of bounds into certain worldly sins that disgrace the Name of the Lord Jesus Christ. They are found in 1 Corinthians 5 and 2 Thessalonians 3. They include such sins as the use of idols and graven images, sexual immorality, stealing, drunkenness, greediness, and railing (defaming) a person's character. Some of these sins might not require discipline until a pattern of behavior develops.

B) The Penalty – The professing believer is now considered a wicked person and is to be taken out of the game, so to speak. That is, he is to be excommunicated from the church fellowship and from even eating in a social way with the other believers. The reason for this is to keep the sin from spreading, as others will fear the consequences of sin. Another reason is for *"the destruction of the flesh"* by delivering *"such a one unto Satan,"* 1 Cor. 5:5. By being cut off from the fellowship of the church, the person now has only the fellowship of Satan's world system left. This is meant to shock and shame him into repenting, thus destroying his fleshly desires.

*"In the name of our Lord Jesus Christ, when ye are gathered together, and my spirit, **with the power of our Lord Jesus Christ...put away** from among yourselves that wicked person,"* 1 Cor. 5:4,13.

If the sinning believer repents, the goal of discipline has been accomplished, which is to receive him back into the bounds of the fellowship **in love**, 2 Cor. 2:8.

C) Preventive Steps – The above step of excommunication is always the last resort. Some milder preventive steps are: personal counsel in meekness, Gal. 6:1; patient teaching, 2 Tim. 2:24; an open and sharp rebuke, 1 Tim. 5:20; Titus 1:13.

So we see there is an inside and an outside to God's local church. The bottom line amazingly is this: **one can be holy enough for heaven but not holy enough for fellowship in God's assembly**. This is so because our acceptability in heaven is based on the cross-work of Jesus Christ, whereas on earth the church is called to witness for God, a witness affected by our works through the Holy Spirit.

#2. Separation from False Teaching

"Let us cleanse ourselves from all filthiness of the flesh and spirit, perfecting holiness in the fear of God." 2 Cor. 7:1

Not only does the Lord want us to be morally separate from the world but also religiously separate. This comes as a surprise to some. But if somebody misrepresents us, making us look bad, we care. So God cares if we misrepresent Him through false teaching. Remember, the church is looked at as a bride and so our loyalty is to Christ and His truth, not to man's religion.

The Penalty for Going Out of Bounds

A) The Charge – When any teacher or group is teaching doctrine that is wrong in relationship to the Person and work of Jesus Christ the Lord and they therefore have "another gospel," they are to be separated from. Contrary to human logic which says to tolerate or to try to help them, the Scriptures command separation rather than weakening yourself and others. It is the rotten apple that affects the rest, not the good apples that change the rotten one.

Notice the teaching from your Lord of how you must stay in bounds and false teachers are to be put out of bounds.

Rom. 16:17,18	False teachers with another gospel	"Avoid them"
1 Tim. 6:3-5	Wrong teachers (money minded)	"Withdraw thyself"
2 Tim. 3:3-5	Those whose lives deny the gospel	"From such turn away"
2 John 7-11	False teachers about Christ	"Receive him not"
2 Cor. 6:17	The religion of unbelievers	"Come out...be separate"
Titus 3:10	One who causes division (heretic)	"Reject"

We see these same principles of God in the Old Testament. In Deuteronomy 13, the children of Israel were to cast out the false prophet.

B) The Penalty - When a professed believer falls into or teaches serious error, the church has authority to stop their mouths and put them out of bounds (excommunication) so others won't be overthrown in their most holy faith. **The false teacher is to be rejected and delivered to Satan,** Titus 1:11; 3:10; 1 Tim. 1:20.

C) Preventive Steps - Some preventive steps are: a clear explanation from the Word of God why they are wrong, taking away their speaking privileges, a sharp rebuke, a warning two times before rejection, Titus 1:9-13; 3:10.

Speaking of religious error against Christ, Hebrews 13:13 says: *"Let us go forth therefore unto him* ***without*** *the camp* [false gospel], *bearing his reproach."* Again, we see an in-bounds and an out-of-bounds.

As we have seen, the church is to judge the sinning believer. God says He will take care of judging the unbeliever – *"them that are without God judgeth,"* but it is the church that is commanded to *"judge them than are within* [believers]," 1 Cor. 5:12,13. If, after the discipline, there is repentance, the believer is to be forgiven, comforted, and taken back into the fellowship in love, 2 Cor. 2:6-11.

The following chart illustrates the process of church judging and discipline.

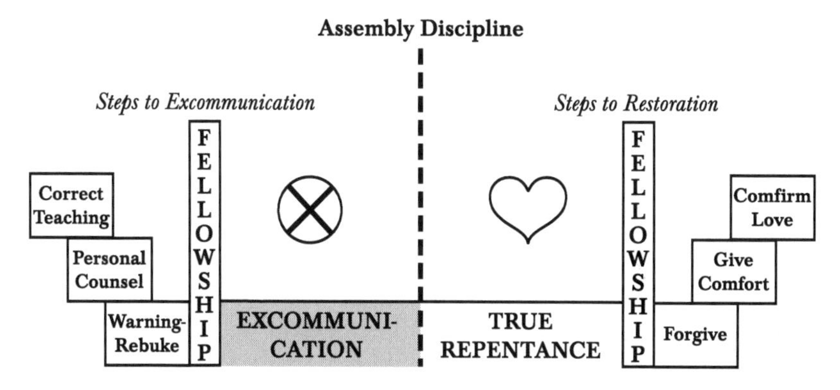

Because the church has boundary lines, the assembly is something definite into which a believer must be received. It has an in-bounds to its fellowship. In Romans 16:1,2 you will observe the practice that, when a believer visited another assembly where he was unknown, a letter of recommendation or introduction was sent with him. This letter informed the church being visited that the believer was in-bounds, and so should be shown Christian love and his spiritual gifts used.

In conclusion, the believer must realize that, although before he was saved he had some sinful habits in his life, God does not expect him to continue in them. This is because the believer now has the power of the Holy Spirit in him, 1 Thess. 4:1-8.

"What then? shall we sin, because we are not under the law, but under grace? ***God forbid.****"* Rom 6:15

Section 10

The Symbolic Commands and the Church

The Disciple's Signs

The word "ordinance" simply means a regulation to be observed. As you know, under the Old Covenant, God gave Israel hundreds of ordinances to keep – from the number of loaves of bread to put on the holy table, to the color of the priests vestments, to the dates of their holy feasts.

Although the church is not under the law, it is not without ordinances, though not nearly as many as Israel had. The apostle tells the believers in 1 Corinthians 11:2, *"**Keep the** **ordinances**, as I delivered them to you."* The word "ordinance" is the Greek word *paradosis* and is translated in the English Bible as either ordinance or tradition. Biblically speaking, it is not a tradition from man but from God, and so is given to be continually obeyed by all the churches. As 2 Thessalonians 2:15 exhorts,

*"Therefore, brethren, stand fast, and **hold the traditions*** [ordinances] *which ye have been taught, whether by word, or our epistle."*

You see, ordinances or traditions are something to be held onto and not to let go.

Though the church has various traditions, including the command to love one another, we want to look at three that involve symbols. That is, they are a regulation or truth to be obeyed by all the churches and involve a symbolic act to convey a picture message. They are:

- **A.** Water Baptism
- **B.** The Lord's Supper or Communion
- **C.** The Head Covering.

A. Water Baptism

Matt. 28:18,19	*"All power is given unto me in heaven and in earth...**baptizing** them in the name of the Father, and of the Son, and of the Holy Ghost."*
Acts 2:41	*"Then they that gladly received his word were **baptized**."*
Acts 8:38	*"They went down both into the water...and he **baptized** him."*
Acts 10:48	*"And he commanded them to be **baptized** in the name of the Lord."*

1. A Symbol of the Gospel

Water baptism symbolizes the death and resurrection of Jesus Christ the Lord. Going into the water shows a death and burial, while coming up out of the water illustrates the rising from the dead. The word baptism conveys the thought of being identified with something or someone. According to Romans 6, the believer is now identifying that sin is wrong and it was dealt with by the death and burial of Jesus Christ in whom the believer's old master (sin, in Adam) was crucified and buried. The believer is now risen with Christ and is alive unto God whom he is pledging to serve and obey as his new master. He is confessing Jesus is Lord!

2. A Command not an Option

Every believer is commanded to be baptized immediately upon being saved. The longest delay of a baptism after conversion recorded in the Bible is 3 days. And that was in the case of the early Christians' number one enemy, Paul. In his case, God had to convince someone that Paul was truly saved and was thus ready to be baptized. Baptism is only commanded for believers – it is never commanded for babies or unbelievers. If a person isn't saved and gets baptized, he just goes into the water a dry sinner and comes out a wet sinner.

From Pentecost (the formation of the church) onward, the Bible knows of no such thing as an unbaptized believer. For that would be like a person saying, "I believe He died for my sins and is risen from the dead as Lord, but I don't plan to obey Him." This is called abominable in Titus 1:16.

Just as a husband wants his wife to wear a wedding ring to show she has forsaken all others and is now identified with him and loves only him, so God wants us to publicly identify with Jesus Christ as Savior and Lord of our lives. Baptism is the symbol that God has ordained to demonstrate identification and love. *"That ye should be married to another"* (namely to Jesus), Rom. 7:4.

3. **A One-Time Act Done First**

Just as the sacrifice of Christ to deal with our sin was a once for all time event never having to be repeated, so water baptism is done only once to the believer upon being born of the Spirit.

Baptism is meant to be the ***first*** step of obedience for the believer as he states in a public confession his identification with the Lord Jesus Christ no matter what the cost. ***The Lord must be first!,*** Luke 14:26. Acts 2:41,42 and all the other baptism verses (Acts 8:12; 10:43-48; 16:15,33; 18:8) show that baptism always came first before becoming part of the local church and partaking of the Lord's Supper. **For, how can one partake of the "*Lord's* Supper" and yet not confess and obey Him as *Lord* in baptism?**

B. The Feast of the Church

The Lord's Supper

"...Eat the Lord's supper...For as often as ye ***eat*** *this bread, and* ***drink*** *this cup, ye do shew the Lord's death till he come."* 1 Cor. 11:20,26

While Israel was given seven major feasts or holy days to be celebrated on specific dates, the church is given only one – the feast of the Lord's Supper, sometimes called communion. Of the seven feasts given to Israel, one was very special and foundational to their history. That feast was Passover, commemorating the night they were delivered from the slavery of Pharaoh and Egypt. They escaped the death judgment of God by applying the blood of the spotless lamb on their individual doors. A new beginning was theirs.

In similar fashion, the church has a feast which is foundational to her new beginning. For the Lord's Supper illustrates how she was delivered from the slavery of Satan and sin, and delivered from the death judgment of God by individual faith in the blood of the spotless Lamb of God, Jesus Christ.

Since the Passover (the shadow) and the Lord's Supper (fulfillment) have similar meanings, we will compare the two to learn about the Lord's Supper.

Passover – It was an ordinance from God Himself and was therefore called "the Lord's Passover." *"And ye shall observe this thing as an ordinance...It is the sacrifice of* ***the LORD'S passover****, who passed over the houses of the children of Israel in Egypt,"* Ex. 12:24,27.

The Lord's Supper – It is an ordinance from the Lord Himself (not from some church or religious council) and therefore it is called "the Lord's Supper." *"Keep the* ***ordinances****, as I delivered them to you... Eat the* ***Lord's supper****...For I have* ***received of the Lord*** *that which also I delivered unto you, that the Lord Jesus the same night in which he was betrayed took bread,"* 1 Cor. 11:2,20,23.

• • • • • • • • • • •

Passover – It was to be a memorial that would cause the future children of Israel to remember their great sacrificial deliverance, thus producing worship to God. *"And this day shall be unto you for a* ***memorial****; and ye shall keep it a feast to the LORD throughout your generations ...That ye shall say, It is the sacrifice of the LORD'S passover...And the people bowed the head and worshiped,"* Ex. 12:14,27.

The Lord's Supper – This is a time of memorial when believers remember the great sacrifice of the Lord Jesus that allowed God's judgment to bypass us. The Lord's Supper can yield **worship** to the One who is **worth it**. *"For even* ***Christ our passover*** *is* ***sacrificed*** *for us: Therefore let us keep the feast...This* [the bread] *is my body, which is broken for you: this do in* ***remembrance*** *of me...This* *cup is the new testament in my blood: this do ye, as oft as ye drink it, in* ***remembrance*** *of me. For as often as ye eat this bread, and drink this cup, ye do shew the Lord's death till he come,"* 1 Cor. 5:7,8; 11:24,25,26.

•••••••••••

Passover - The feast consisted of only three things: the slain roasted spotless lamb, bitter herbs, and unleavened bread, Ex. 12:8. For the following 7 days, no leaven (yeast) whatsoever was to be in the bread. One who did allow leaven was to be cut off from Israel *"Ye shall keep it a* ***feast*** *by an ordinance forever. Seven days shall ye eat* ***unleavened*** *bread; even the first day ye shall* ***put away leaven*** *out of your houses: for whosoever eateth leavened bread from the first day until the seventh day,* ***that soul shall be cut off from Israel,"*** Ex. 12:14,15.

The Lord's Supper - This feast consists of three items, two physical and one spiritual: **One**, the loaf of bread which when broken symbolizes the body of the spotless Lamb of God slain on the cross; **Two**, the cup of the fruit of the vine which symbolizes the bitter sufferings of our Lord as He shed His blood in a violent death, 1 Cor. 11; and **Three**, the believer's holy lives referred to as the absence of leaven. This does not necessarily mean the absence of literal leaven (yeast) in this loaf of bread ***but the absence of sin in the lives of the believers*** who are keeping the feast. Sin is likened to leaven for it spreads if not purged out. A believer who continues in certain sins (leaven) is to be excommunicated.

"Know ye not that a little leaven leaveneth the whole lump? Purge out therefore the old leaven, that ye may be a new lump, ***as ye are unleavened****. For even* ***Christ our passover*** *is sacrificed for us: Therefore let us keep the feast,* ***not with old leaven****, neither with the leaven of malice and wickedness; but with the unleavened bread of sincerity and truth...* ***Therefore put away from among yourselves that wicked person,"*** 1 Cor. 5:6-8,13.

•••••••••••

WARNING This is the one meeting of the church that requires that each person examine himself to discern the deep significance of the Lord's body and blood. A violation of this sacred time can bring chastening from the Lord to the point of death, 1 Cor. 11:27-32.

Passover – In its immediate context, Passover was given to Israel to be kept forever. However, Israel broke the covenant with God and so He spoke of a New Covenant that would come, Jer. 31:31-34. This great reformation occurred at the coming and crucifixion of Jesus Christ. And so in the mind of God, the ordinance of Passover was to last only until the coming of Christ. *"Which was a figure for the time then present, in which were offered both gifts and sacrifices...* ***Which stood*** *only in meats and drinks, and divers washings, and carnal* ***ordinances,*** *imposed on them* ***until the time of reformation****. But* ***Christ being come...****"* Heb. 9:9-11.

The Lord's Supper – This feast also is a temporary one, for it only stands until Christ comes again. Then we will see Him face to face and there will be no need to remember. *"For as often as ye eat this bread, and drink this cup, ye do shew the Lord's death till he come,"* 1 Cor. 11:26.

• • • • • • • • • • •

Passover – It was a feast to be observed repeatedly by the whole congregation collectively. Once every year, on the 14th day in the evening of the first month of Israel's religious calendar, this feast was to be kept. *"In the* ***first month, on the fourteenth day of the month*** *at even, ye shall eat unleavened bread, until the one and twentieth day of the month at even,"* Ex. 12:18.

The Lord's Supper – It too is to be kept on a repeated basis; however, there are no specific dates given other than **often**. *"For as* ***often*** *as ye eat this bread, and drink this cup, ye do shew the Lord's death,"* 1 Cor. 11:26.

Upon studying the New Testament, you will discover that the Lord's Supper was the central reason for the meeting of the church. **The primary reason for their assembling together was to worship and remember the Lord through the feast of the Lord's Supper.**

This is first love. It was not kept on an individual basis, but when the church assembled collectively. Other activities were important but they flowed from this. Consider the following reports:

Acts 2:42 *"And they **continued steadfastly** in the apostles' doctrine and fellowship, and **in breaking of bread*** **[i.e., Lord's Supper]**, *and in prayers."*

Acts 2:46 *"And they, **continuing daily** with one accord in the temple, and **breaking bread** from house to house..."*

Acts 20:7 *"And upon **the first day of the week**, when the disciples came together **to break bread**, Paul preached unto them."*

1 Cor. 10:16; 16:2 *"**The bread which we break**, is it not the communion of the body of Christ?...Upon the **first day** of the week..."* (The latter verse is used to show this was the assembling day of the Corinthian church, and according to chapter 11, they always celebrated this feast when they assembled together in one place. Regrettably there was disorder which Paul wrote to correct.)

So, the Lord's Supper observance ranges from a daily basis to the first day of every week which is referred to by Christians as the Lord's Day, for that is the day He was risen to reign. The record of once a week is the least you will find it in the Scriptures. Could the Lord have left the frequency of this feast in a liberty area to test us to see how much we love Him?

C. The Head Covering

"Let her [the woman] *be covered. For a man indeed ought not to cover his head." 1 Cor. 11:6,7*

This symbol is a surprise to some, but it is in the Bible as a command to the church. Head-covering symbolizes a colossal truth of God – submission to authority. In a Satanic age that rebels against authority whether to parents or to government, what a magnificent way this is for the church to demonstrate agreement with God's authority structure!

Although many have claimed that this passage was just for the Corinthian church of that day because of cultural prostitution problems, an honest evaluation of the context teaches the opposite. It is for all churches everywhere. Notice that the scope of the apostle's teaching extends beyond the Corinthian church to all churches.

1 Cor. 1:2 *"Unto the church of God which is at Corinth...with **all that in every place** call upon the name of Jesus Christ our Lord."*

1 Cor. 4:17 *"My **ways** which be in Christ, as **I teach every where in every church.**"*

1 Cor. 7:17 *"And so ordain I in **all** churches."*

1 Cor. 11:16 [Regarding the non use of head-covering] *"We have no such custom, neither the **churches** of God."*

1 Cor. 14:33,34 *"For God is not the author of confusion, but of peace, as in **all** churches of the saints. Let your women keep silence in the **churches.**"*

The reason for the head-covering symbol

1 Cor. 11:3 *"But I would have you **know**, that the **head** of every man is Christ; and the **head** of the woman is the man; and the **head** of Christ is God."*

God is teaching headship. Notice His ordained order of authority was established by creative choice and not by the dictates of Corinthian culture. Remember, that to accomplish our salvation even Christ submitted Himself to the will and headship of God.

When is the covering to be in effect?

1 Cor. 11:4,5 *"Every **man praying or prophesying**, having his head covered, dishonoureth his head* [Christ]. *But **every woman that prayeth or prophesieth** with her head uncovered dishonoureth her head* [the man].

Since man is the God-ordained head in the man-woman relationship, he is to not put anything over his head when speaking to God or from God. Man is thus stating there is no head over him on earth. Therefore, he is responsible to lead the woman in the ways of his Head who is in heaven, the Lord Jesus Christ. **The woman does the exact opposite**. When speaking **to** God or **from** God she is to put something ***over*** her head, showing that, though she is in God's presence, she is submitting to God's authority which places the man ***over*** her.

Why The Difference?

verses 7-10

Man Uncovered	*Woman Covered*
Man is for God's Glory *"For a man indeed ought not to cover his head, forasmuch as he is the image and glory of God,"* 1 Cor. 11:7.	**Woman is the glory of the man** *"But the woman is the glory of the man,"* 1 Cor. 11:7. Thus, she veils herself in the presence of God, agreeing she is the glory of man rather than God's glory.
The Man came first *"For the* ***man*** *is not of the woman"* (Adam came first in order), 1 Cor. 11:8. Thus, by not putting anything over his head, man is agreeing that he, by being first, is the head of the woman and responsible to lead.	**The Woman came second** *"But the* ***woman*** [is] *of the man"* (the woman by coming from the man was second in order), 1 Cor. 11:8. Thus, by putting something over her head she is agreeing that the man is first and is over her as her head.
Man NOT created for the woman *"Neither was the* ***man*** *created for the woman,"* 1 Cor. 11:9. Man leaves himself uncovered in the presence of God, and thereby acknowledges his direct role in creation – for God.	**Woman WAS created for the man** *"But the* ***woman*** [created] *for the man,"* 1 Cor. 11:9. The woman was specifically created to be a suitable helper fit for man, Gen. 2:18. By covering her head she is veiling herself in the presence of God, thus agreeing with her creation purpose – for the man.

Man – cont'd **No authority-sign on his head**	***Woman – cont'd*** **Authority-sign on her head**
"For a man indeed ought not to cover his head," 1 Cor. 11:7. Man, by leaving his head uncovered is agreeing that there is no woman in authority **over** him as he is the authority of God in the man-woman relationship.	*"For this cause ought the woman to have power* [authority] *on her head because of the angels,"* 1 Cor. 11:10. By covering her head, she is showing the angels, who are learning the wisdom of God, that there is an authority **over** her, the man, in God's sovereign plan.

The covering actually symbolizes the man. Notice she does not put it under her feet claiming to be over him, nor does she put it by her side, claiming equality in authority. Rather she covers her head, showing she is submitting to the man who is over her. Does all the above evidence sound like Corinthian culture or Creator choices? Consider the angel factor also, if you believe this is just a cultural thing.

Should the man act superior?

1 Cor. 11:11-12 Absolutely not! The apostle cautions the man against abusing this authority when he reminds him that man now comes from the woman and so in the Lord they need each other. Headship is a responsibility in love. Remember, man also has a head, the Lord Jesus Christ, and he is to lead the woman in **His** ways, not according to his own personal desires.

Nature adds its Amen

1 Cor. 11:13-15 In these verses, the apostle appeals to nature itself to help us understand the difference between the man and woman. Naturally, man is meant to have short hair, as long hair is a shame to him. On the contrary, the woman is meant to have long hair, as that is her glory. Being shorn would be to her shame. So, nature itself, by making the woman attractive with long hair, has also provided a covering for the woman in a natural way.

This fact of nature is meant to add support to the head-covering teaching the Lord just gave in verses 1-12, rather than to replace it. If her long hair was the only covering referred to, it would be quite impossible to take it off when she was finished praying or prophesying and then to put it on when she is ready to pray again.

Also, the Greek word in verse 15 for nature's covering is *peribolaion*, while the Greek word for the veil covering in verse 6 is *katakalupto,* which, by the way, means to hide from view or cover wholly.

Conclusion

1 Cor. 11:16

In verse 16, the apostle concludes by teaching that if one is inclined to argue about it, the churches of God have no other way of doing it than what he just taught. Would to God that was still true today. Also, in 1 Corinthians 14:37, Paul claims that the things he writes are *"the commandments of the Lord."*

Is this such a hard thing to obey for the One who shed His blood for you in love?

Section 11

The Role of Male and Female in The Church

The Disciple's Obedience

As is obvious in a physical sense, God has made men and women differently. Each has different inborn capabilities to perform best within his or her God-given roles. When they step out of their created roles, it is like being a fish out of water. There will be pressures and problems that they will face unnecessarily and they will find they are not "programmed" to handle them over a period of time.

From the beginning in Genesis, the sovereign God created woman specifically to be a help meet, or fit, for man. The woman was designed to complement and support the man, a very high and important calling. Remember, the fall into sin was the result of Eve's stepping out of her role, acting as the head, and making a spiritual decision apart from her husband. Therefore, she ended up being deceived.

After the fall of Adam and Eve, God more clearly defined the male and female roles. To the woman He said, *"Thy desire shall be to thy husband, and he shall rule over thee..."* Gen. 3:16. The woman's main role would be connected with bearing children, keeping the home, and honoring her husband. The man was appointed as head, provider or breadwinner. This would not be accomplished without much sweat and hard work. Thus, their roles are different.

Warning Different does not mean unequal in value or importance. A stove and refrigerator are definitely different but still equal in importance to the operation of a kitchen. When their important differences are utilized, a successful meal is the result. When men and women reverse their different roles, great problems are encountered.

Following is a chart of 8 major differences that God has ordained between men and women.

DIFFERENCE	*Man*	***Woman***	Verses
1. Physical (hair)	*Short*	***Long***	1 Cor. 11:14,15
2. Manner of Creation	*From Dust*	***From Rib***	Gen. 2
3. Purpose of Creation	*For glory of God*	***Glory and helper of Man***	1 Cor. 11:7-9
4. Child Bear-ing role	*Has Seed and is Provider*	***The bearer/ keeps home***	Titus 2:3-5
5. Authority	*Head – Loving Leader*	***Submissive in reverence***	Eph. 5:21-33
6. Emotionally	*Stronger vessel – tough*	***Weaker vessel – tender***	1 Pet. 3:1-7
7. Spiritual role in God's Church	*Vocal, Leadership*	***Silent, no leadership***	1 Tim. 2; 1 Cor. 14
8. Head-covering	*Uncovered*	***Covered***	1 Cor. 11:1-16

Since God has ordained differences between man and woman in nature and in the home, it should not surprise us to see differences in their roles in the church of God.

The Differences in God's Church

The woman's role is supportive, non-authoritative and silent when the assembly meets.

> 1 Cor. 14:26,34,35 – *"How is it then, brethren? When ye* ***come together****...Let your women keep* ***silence*** *in the churches:* ***for it is not permitted unto them to speak****; but they*

> *are commanded to be* ***under obedience*** *as also saith the law. And if they will learn any thing, let them ask their husbands at home:* ***for it is a shame for women to speak in the church.****"*

> 1 Tim. 2:11-14 – *"Let the woman* ***learn in silence*** *with all subjection. But I suffer* [permit] *not a woman to* ***teach****, nor to* ***usurp authority*** *over the man, but to be in* ***silence****. For Adam was first formed, then Eve. And Adam was not deceived, but the woman being deceived was in the transgression."*

> So the woman's role will not include holding a leadership position, nor teaching a man, nor even asking a question, which is what a learner does. It is a role of silent subjection. Notice carefully that God does not base this on the culture of that day but on His choice in creation and the woman's deception in the fall. This is also demonstrated in the law. For in the law there was never a female king, priest, Levite temple officer, or Levite choir singer ordained by God.

The man's role is vocal and involves leadership.

> The verses and the context show that the man's role is exactly opposite for it is vocal and involves leadership. The Christian man, who believes God, will take this responsibility seriously and be in the Word so he can minister to the church. He should also be open to the heavy responsibility and problems of leadership as God calls.

God's Good Works for a Christian Woman

God is not saying a woman isn't valuable and important, but He is saying He created her with a tender touch and has placed her in a different, but necessary, role. 1 Timothy 5:10 states that a woman should be well reported of for *"good works."* The following is a list of God's definition of *"good works."* After viewing this list and how the woman adds the tender touch to the body (something a man can't do nearly as well), one can never say that the woman is unimportant in God's plan.

Good Works

• Bring up precious children	1 Tim. 5:14
• Using the home as a little mission to lodge strangers	1 Tim. 5:10
• Washing the saints' feet (deeds of mercy)	1 Tim. 5:10
• Relieving the afflicted (tender touch)	1 Tim. 5:10
• Loving and standing behind her husband	Titus 2:5
• Hospitality to God's family	1 Pet. 4:9
• Prayer	Acts 16:13
• Prophesying (outside a church meeting)	Acts 21:9
• Practical service in the assembly	Rom. 16:1
• Spiritual worship	John 4:24
• Witnessing in evangelism	Acts 8:4
• Teaching and guiding the younger women as godly homemakers	Titus 2:3-5
• Setting an example of purity	Titus 2:3,5
• Living lesson to the angels on subjection	1 Cor. 11:10

It is these very "good works" that God says should be the Christian woman's jewelry or adornment. *"That women **adorn** themselves...(which becometh women professing godliness) with **good works**,"* 1 Tim. 2:9,10. *"The **ornament** of a meek and quiet spirit, which is in the sight of God of great price,"* 1 Pet. 3:4. This should be the adornment of the godly woman rather than the costly clothing, gold, pearls, and plaited hair which typify a worldly woman. God loves the *"shamefaced"* look (reverent, modest, or bashful) rather than the bold sensuous look, 1 Tim. 2:9.

Yes, the woman's main sphere of activity is guiding the home, not leadership in the church as an elder or teacher.

> "[Women] *to be discreet, chaste, **keepers at home**, good, obedient to their own husbands, that the word of God be not blas-*

> *phemed,"* Titus 2:5. *"She looketh well to the ways of her* ***house-hold...*** *"* Prov. 31:27.

Don't let Satan and the world system trick you into underestimating the woman's role. It is the highest career a woman could have and God calls it a jewel of "great price," 1 Pet. 3:4.

As the USA and Canada are abandoning God's roles, it's not hard to understand why the family is breaking apart. As the number of working mothers climbs, so do the statistics of divorce and child problems. Is this a coincidence or is it an effect of stepping out of God's wise plan? Don't let Satan bait you with a few extra material items that will also pose a threat to your family serenity now and rob you of eternal rewards as your Savior is grieved.

WARNING Christian husbands, remember you are responsible to lead and encourage your wife in these areas and to love her as you would your own body.

The Mark of True Spirituality

It is important to notice that after the apostle is finished talking about head-covering, the Lord's Supper, the orderly use of gifts in a meeting, and the woman's silence, he states; *"If any man think himself to be a prophet, or* ***spiritual****, let him* ***acknowledge*** *that the things that I write unto you are* ***the commandments of the Lord,"*** 1 Cor. 14:37.

The bottom line of spirituality in God's eyes is not how much gift you have or how many souls you win or how many people attend or even how happy you are, but it is obedience to His Word! Verse 38 teaches that if one claims to be a prophet or spiritual person and does not submit to these commandments, he is to be ignored as such and not recognized or trusted in such a claim. This is a safeguard for knowing whom you should follow.

Let's give God credit for His superior wisdom in the differences between the sexes and simply yield to Him.

Section 12

CHURCH GOVERNMENT: GOD'S STYLE

The Disciple's Leaders

As we continue, you might have already found some of the truth presented non-traditional (unconventional). But the question is not, Is it non-traditional? but, Is it Scriptural? The Lord Jesus asks the question in Matthew 15:3, *"Why do ye transgress the commandment of God by your **tradition**?"*

Thus, in the pursuit of Scriptural truth over tradition, we continue with the subject of church government. With countless varieties of churches existing today, God still has His plan for His church and it still works for the glory of God. There are two main distinctions between tradition and Scripture on the vital subject of governing a church. They are as follows:

#1. The Location of Headquarters

God's design for His church has no human head or headquarters on this earth. However, the church does have a head or headquarters but it is unseen as our head is the living Lord Jesus Christ headquartered now in heaven. Nothing could be more explicit.

Eph. 1:22,23 — *"And gave him to be the **head** over **all things** to the church, which is his body."*

Eph. 5:23,24 — *"Christ is the **head** of the church...Therefore as the church is **subject** unto Christ..."*

Col. 1:18 — *"And he is the **head** of the body, the church...that in all things he might have the preeminence."*

In the Bible, each local assembly of believers was autonomous.

That means that each was self-governed and independent of the control of another assembly or hierarchy. Each was answerable for its actions to the Head, the Lord Jesus. Although many concerned elders met in Jerusalem under the apostles (Acts 15) to deal with the doctrine of the true gospel, no precedent or subsequent teaching was given to the churches to form a central authority on earth. The seven churches found in Revelation 2 and 3 show autonomy and Christ's headship in action; each individual assembly was told, *"He that hath an ear, let him hear what the Spirit saith unto the churches."*

When Paul the Apostle announced to the Ephesian elders that they would see his face no more, one might ask to what authority would the church now look? The answer is given in Acts 20:32: *"And now, brethren, I commend you to God, and to the word of his grace, which is able to build you up."* God and the Scriptures were now their authority.

The wisdom of God's plan is that if, for example, an earthly human headquarters controls five hundred churches, all Satan must do is concentrate on its headquarters. Once he corrupts that, the five hundred churches under it could easily go down in a fairly short period of time. Church history has clearly demonstrated this in the denominations. But if five hundred churches are only holding to the untouchable and unseen Head in heaven, which is beyond Satan's reach and power, he now must concentrate on all five hundred. The job is now far more difficult and much less possible.

God's master design keeps His church from being super-organized and centralized in human power. Thus, the church is able to go underground quickly and survive, as it has done. In this sense a local church is portable as it operates only on the power of the Holy Spirit, the only vicar God recognizes to represent the Head on earth.

Local churches could be compared to several portable tape recorders that each operates on its own permanent internal battery power, independent of any outside power source. If the main electrical power of a building is short circuited or damaged, the tape recorders continue working correctly because they are each independent of the central power source in the building.

WARNING Although the Scriptures show autonomy for the local church in liberating it from other human authorities, it never promotes independence from the fellowship of other believers. Rather it exhorts all churches in the responsibility to receive and edify the weaker brother, to recognize Scriptural discipline when carried out by another assembly, to use the gifts of the whole body. For remember, *"There is one body."*

The Church's only Head –	***The Lord Jesus***
The Church's only Guide on earth –	***The Holy Spirit***
The Church's only Authority –	***The Holy Scriptures***

#2. Elders and Deacons as the Only Governing Positions

Philippians 1:1 reveals 3 types of work in God's church

1 **"To all the saints in Christ Jesus"** - every believer with his/her individual gifts to use.

2 **"with the bishops"** - *'episkopos'* in the Greek, translated overseer or bishop and is synonymous with the word 'elder'; one who sees over the spiritual condition of the flock and who feeds it.

3 **"and deacons"** - a servant; one who serves, in a recognized public way, the physical need of the assembly.

The work of an overseer-elder and of a deacon are the only two work-positions in the church for which qualifications are given, 1 Tim. 3; Titus 1. Upon attentive reading of Acts 20:17-32, you will find that elders and overseers (bishops) are exactly the same. All other offices such as cardinal, archbishop, president, pastor, etc., are man-made and have no qualifications to be found for them in the Word of God.

Elders – In God's plan, He has entrusted the Head's Word to spiritually gifted and qualified human leadership. However, the elders are never given the authority to create new rules or to change God's ordinances, but by example and word they are to teach the Head's Word to the flock.

> **WARNING** Eldership is not a factory to manufacture new truth, but a safety deposit box to preserve the original truths so they can be passed on in their original form, 2 Tim. 2:2. Also, the church is not intended to be a democracy where the majority vote rules, but a theocracy where the Lord rules through elders who communicate His Word.

Upon studying the Scriptures, it is evident that the elders do not have all the gifts nor are they expected to do everything (this is a clergy - laity concept). Although there are many secondary roles that may arise through circumstances for the elder, the Bible teaches three main functions of elders in a local assembly. We believe elders are performing their role if they accomplish these three.

1. **To rule or guide the sheep in the ways of God.**
   This will involve spiritual discernment and saying "yes" or "no" to certain things. The word "overseer", Acts 20:28, means to see over and ensure the correct progress of the flock. While not lording it over the sheep, the elders will rule or take care of the house of God, 1 Tim. 3:5; 5:17.

2. **To feed the sheep the pure Word of God.**
   Through teaching the Bible, to ensure that the flock is given the opportunity to receive much correct Bible instruction. Such teaching is to be backed up by a life that is an example. This teaching is to exhort or rebuke the sheep in the ways of God with all authority, Acts 20:28,32; 1 Pet. 5:1-5; Titus 2:15.

3. **To guard and protect the sheep from false teachers and erring doctrine.**

To be able to identify the false and refute it clearly with Scripture. To deal with erring teachers, and when the sheep are being misled, to stop with Scripture the mouths of those who are in error, Acts 20:29,30; Titus 1:9-14. This might involve sharp rebuking or rejection after two warnings, Titus 3:10.

The Scriptures teach that elders are to be obeyed and submitted to. Also, they are to be highly esteemed in love and given double honor (financial if necessary) when they do their job well. Some will be better at ruling while others will specialize in teaching. No accusation should ever be received against an elder unless there are at least two or three witnesses, 1 Tim. 5:17-21; Heb. 13:17; 1 Thess. 5:13,14.

WARNING Submission means to "stay under" while pride means to "lift up". The proud, instead of staying under and obeying, exalt themselves up to the elders' authority and do it their own way. Submission isn't just obeying when those in authority agree with you but must encompass all areas. *"**Submit** yourselves unto the elder...for God resisteth the **proud**, and giveth grace to the **humble**,"* 1 Pet. 5:5.

It is the Holy Spirit who makes one an elder. If the man meets the qualifications, he should have liberty to function as an overseer whether he is a professional with a seminary degree or not. However, an elder is not to lord it over the flock; he is not to dictate every move, but rather by clear Scripture and by a holy example and loving kindness, he is to lead the flock in ways that glorify God.

The work of an overseer is not popular today with our anti-authority mind set. Also, it is not glamorous in this day of para-church organizations with their presidents, executive directors, chancellors, professors, etc., but God calls it both a *"good work"* and one to be desired. God Himself will reward the faithful overseeing shepherds with a *"crown of glory"* in that future day, 1 Pet. 5:4.

The difference between an elder's and a deacon's work (the only two "offices" in the church) can be seen in the differences in their qualifications as the following chart illustrates:

ELDERS	DEACONS
Character	***Character***
Serious minded - (worthy of respect)	*Serious minded - (worthy of respect)*
Not controlled by wine	*Not controlled by wine*
Not a lover of money or covetous of things	*Not a lover of money*
Good report - Above blame	*Good report and blameless*
Good behavior	*Not a double talker -*
A lover of good	*(his word is trustworthy)*
Marital	***Marital***
Husband of one wife	*Husband of one wife*
Faithful family	*Faithful family*
Doctrinal	***Doctrinal***
Holding fast the faithful word	*Holding the mystery of the faith*
Administrative	***Administrative***
Rule family and house well	*Rule family and house well*
Time	***Time***
Not a beginner - (novice)	*Not a beginner - first proved*
Teaching	-------
Ability to teach	
Skilled in doctrine (thus able to exhort the sheep and convince the contradictors)	
People Qualities	-------
Loving hospitality	
Not quarrelsome or a brawler	
Patient, gentle, and peaceable	
Not self-willed or stubborn	
Not quick tempered	
Not combative with physical blows	
Self-controlled	
Just	

Deacons – The deacon is one who will serve in practical areas such as finances, maintenance, etc. The deacon must meet certain qualifications and is to be proven first. His job is valuable to the functioning of the assembly and should be done well, 1 Tim. 3:8-13; Phil. 1:1. His job may be determined by circumstances and by the elders of the assembly, Acts 6.

The Plurality of Elders in Every Local Church

The Bible knows nothing of one man teaching and governing the assembly. God's plan is to have a plurality of elders for every church. God's wisdom in having a plurality of leader-teachers (elders) in each local assembly can be seen in not putting all the power, teaching, and tremendous responsibility into the hands of one man. Instead, each balances and helps the other in giving the flock the time and variety of teaching it needs.

If a church is dependent upon only one teacher and he fails or leaves, the church usually suffers too. But where there is a plurality of leadership, if Satan stumbles one, the other elders are still there to preserve the flock in a check and balance system. Church history has clearly validated this wisdom. Isn't it good to have a Head who is smarter than we are, whose wisdom can be trusted?

The Bible clearly reveals this plurality of elder-teachers for each church.

Acts 11:30	*"And sent it to the **elders*** [of the church at Jerusalem]*."*
Acts 13:1	*"Now there were in the church that was at Antioch certain prophets and **teachers**."*
Acts 20:17	*"He sent to Ephesus, and called the **elders** of the church."*
Titus 1:5	*"Ordain **elders** in every city."*
James 5:14	*"Is any sick among you? let him call for the **elders** of the church."*
Acts 14:23	*"And when they had ordained them **elders in every church**."*

Acts 15:35 *"Paul also and Barnabas continued in Antioch, teaching and preaching the word of the Lord, with many others also."*

What about the Office of the Pastor?

Many Christian churches think of a pastor as a professional, a seminary graduate who is hired to do the majority of the pulpit teaching, including preaching the gospel, visiting the sick, counselling the hurting, etc. He is usually considered the main leader of the church and responsible for many decisions made. Have you ever wondered why such a high and responsible office as this has **no stated qualifications** in the N.T.? Remember, there are only qualifications for the elders and the deacons.

The simple answer is that the office of a pastor didn't exist in the N.T. pattern. As has been demonstrated, the Bible knows only of a plurality of elder-teachers for each church. However, the N.T. does speak of pastors, but never as an office. **Rather it is a gift** that some have for the perfecting of the church – *"and gave **gifts** unto men...And he gave some...pastors,"* Eph. 4:8,11. The word pastor in the Greek is *poimeen* and is translated "shepherd" or "shepherds" seventeen times and "pastors" (which means shepherds) once, in Ephesians 4:11, in which it is labeled a **gift** that some have. A person with the **gift** of pastoring might not have the gift of the evangelist or the gift of showing mercy or the gift of helps, etc., and therefore he can't do everything.

A person with the **gift** of pastoring will have supernatural ability to shepherd (i.e., feed and guide the flock). Thus, the leadership of a church is designed to be made up of **elders**, who not only meet the character qualifications but possess the ability to shepherd because of the **gift** of pastoring which the Holy Spirit has given them, Acts 20:28. However, it is possible to have the gift of pastoring but not be an elder because of not meeting the 21 qualifications. (Since a gift is simply a spiritual talent given by God, character qualifications don't enter into it.) But, every true overseer-elder will have the gift of shepherding or pastoring. For example, one could say that all doctors must have medical knowledge, but not all people with medical knowledge are doctors.

The only Senior or Chief Pastor (singular) whom God acknowledges for His church is the Lord Jesus Christ: *"When the chief Shepherd* [*poimeen* – pastor] *shall appear,"* 1 Pet. 5:4.

Some are under the impression that Timothy and Titus were "the pastor" of their local churches. That is not so if we examine the Holy Scriptures. They were apostolic delegates, i.e., assistants and fellow workers with Paul. They were commissioned and given authority by the apostle to travel to various churches to correct problems and to teach the apostles' doctrine, etc. At times they were to ordain elders (overseers or bishops) in each assembly as they continued with God's master design. Their job was to work themselves out of a job and then to move on to another area. (Examine 1 Cor. 4:17; 2 Cor. 8:23; Titus 1:5; 2 Tim. 1:3; Acts 16:3; Rom. 16:21.)

WARNING Because God is very merciful with His people, do not look at other true Christian churches as being of Satan because they might be governed by the office of a one-man pastor with possibly an assistant. Study 1 Samuel 8, 10, and 12 and you will discover the longsuffering of God as He permitted Israel to have a one-man monarchy to lead them in place of judges and elders. And there were some godly kings such as David. Although it wasn't God's directive will, He permitted His people to have it their way. Thus, godly Samuel would not forsake God's people with their king because God did not. But, also remember where the kings eventually led Israel: to *apostasy*. God's directive will is always the best.

May God help us to be not only fundamental but also governmental, i.e., following God's pattern of guiding the flock in our local assemblies.

1. Corporate Church Government

Man's Tradition

God's Pattern

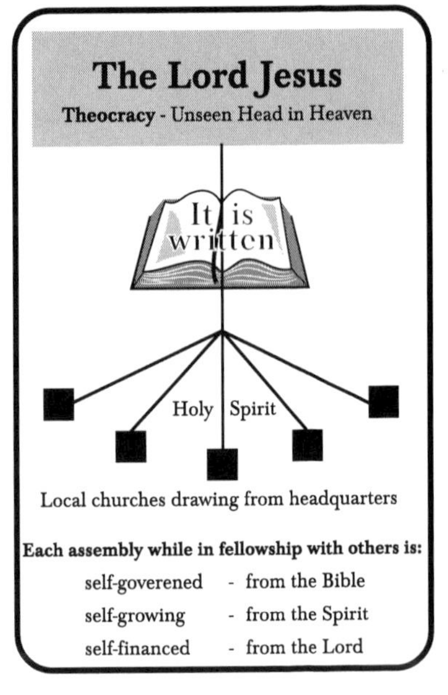

2. Local Church Government

Man's Tradition

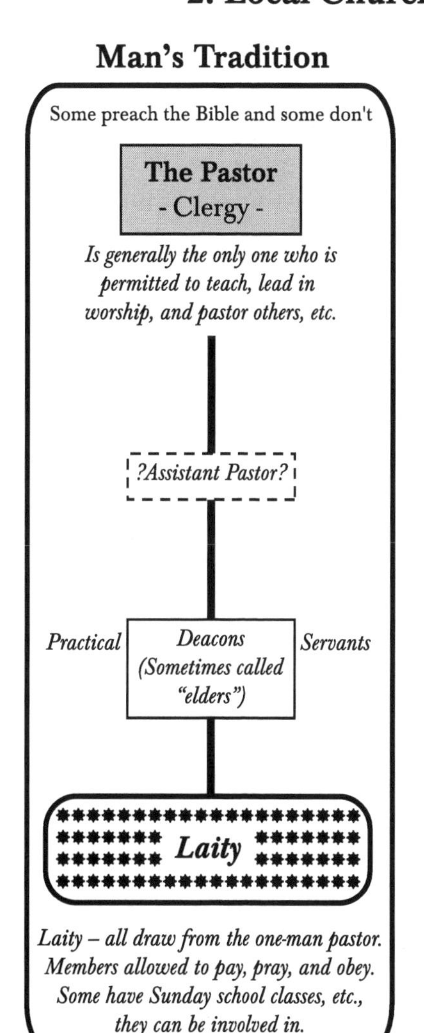

God's Pattern

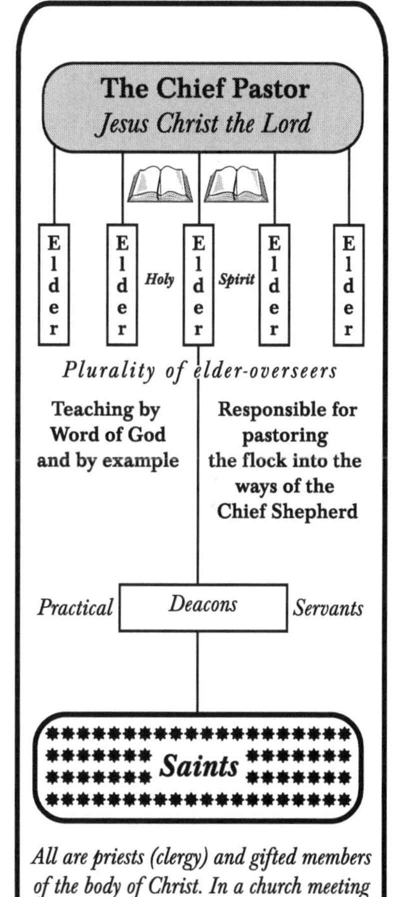

Section 13

THE PRIESTHOOD OF THE CHURCH

The Disciple's Calling

Although every believer will not be doing the work (office) of an elder or deacon, each one is equally a priest. Therefore, every believer should be involved in an internal way in the church's worship and service to God. This is a radical new truth in the N.T.

Old Testament Way

In the O.T., only one out of the twelve tribes of the children of Israel was constituted priests. This was the tribe of Levi. Only the Levite priests were permitted to offer sacrifices, to eat the most holy things, to enter the holy sanctuary to offer the incense of worship, and to instruct the people from the law. (Sometimes they would teach from an elevated wooden pulpit - the priests would teach and the people would listen, Neh. 8.) The priests were financially supported by the non-priestly tribes. Thus, the select tribe of Levi was *clergy*, and the non-priestly tribes were the common people or *laity*. The priests could be identified as clergy by their special religious vestments. (Study Num. 18, Ezek. 44, etc.)

Thus while the clergy (priests) served exclusively in the house of God, the common people (laity) held secular jobs in Israel and their primary duty regarding the house of God was to pay, pray, and obey.

However, this is not the way it is in the New Testament church, though many still traditionally gravitate to the old legalistic way. Unmistakably absent in the N.T. are any instructions for religious vestments, for selected duties, or for exclusive rights for a separate priestly caste called clergy. This is because in the church there are no longer any clergy and laity distinctions, for by the grace of the gospel of Jesus Christ – ***every believer is now constituted a priest.***

Thus, there is no longer any need for holy vestments for a special class because all believers are equally holy in Christ. There is no need for special titles such as *"reverend", "father", "Rabbi",* (teacher) *"master"*, because now the Lord Himself is the believer's only father, master, and teacher, and we are all equally "brethren" in the family of God. (See Ps. 111:9 KJV; Matt. 23:7-10; Gal. 3:26-28.)

You should also notice in the N.T. epistles, no believer is ever addressed by his particular gift such as "Giving Gwen" or "Showing Mercy Mike" or "Helper Helen" or "Evangelist Ernie" or "Teacher Ted" or "Pastor so and so." This is because of the priesthood of all believers and because a gift is something we have received from God. 1 Corinthians 4:7 asks, *"Now if thou didst receive it, why dost thou glory?"*

Note – The New Testament terms for followers of the Lord Jesus Christ:

believer	2 times
saints	62 times
brethren	232 times
Christian	3 times
disciples	31 times
priests	5 times

Yes, in the New Testament we learn the radical news: *"for the priesthood being changed..."* Heb. 7:12. This important change not only recognizes Jesus Christ as our permanent High Priest and only intercessor with God, but it makes every believer equally a priest. Every believer now has direct access to the Lord without any human mediator, 1 Tim. 2:5; Rom. 5:2; Eph. 2:18. The New Testament tells all believers:

> 1 Pet. 2:5 – *"Ye also, as lively stones, are built up a spiritual house, an holy priesthood, to offer up spiritual sacrifices, acceptable to God by Jesus Christ."*
>
> 1 Pet. 2:9 – *"But ye are a chosen generation, a royal priesthood, an holy nation, a peculiar people; that ye should shew forth the praises of him who hath called you out of darkness into his marvelous light."*

But one might ask, how is one made a priest? By an ordination ceremony? By graduating from seminary? No, but by being made holy by the precious blood of Jesus. *"Unto him that loved us, and washed us from our sins in his own blood, and hath* ***made us*** *kings and priests unto God and his Father..."* Rev. 1:5,6. Therefore, clergy and laity distinctions do not exist in the N.T. **for we are all clergy**, we are all priests.

Priests and the Church Meeting

Upon observing how the early church functioned in its meetings, it is obvious that the priesthood of all believers was more than just a doctrine to be held; it was a vital truth to be practiced. Visible expression was given to this new way. A brother did not just come to church to listen, but he came spiritually exercised to give edification to the body. This method designed by God helps develop spiritual gift rather than it lying dormant while "the clergy" does it all. Just like an athlete – if he doesn't exercise and practice, he will not be sharp – so a believer who cannot or does not use what God gave him will be weak and rusty.

A Visit to a N.T. Assembly Meeting

Let's walk in and visit the Corinthian assembly after they responded to Paul's correction. If you are sitting in your pew waiting for the pastor to get up and preach the sermon for the week and then go home, you are in for a surprise.

One brother offers up a prayer.

2 or 3 brothers give a teaching.

One brother offers up a spiritual song.

Another brother gives a psalm of praise.

Others have liberty to use their gift in an orderly fashion to edify the body.

The Lord Jesus is the authority via His written commandments, 1 Cor. 14:37, and the enabler is the Holy Spirit, 1 Cor. 12. Believe it or not, the Bible states the result of this is *"that all may learn, and all may be comforted,"* 1 Cor. 14:31.

This pattern allows the church to be exposed to the maximum of variety and gift, and allows the Spirit to freshly minister to His church.

WARNING It is also true that all believers do not have the same gifts, as will be discussed in more detail in the next section, so all shouldn't be doing the same things (such as teaching, etc.).

In light of what we have learned so far, the following should characterize a biblical local church.

- The local church will have no outside authority except the Head in heaven, the Lord Jesus.
- A plurality of overseer-elders will lead the flock with the Word of God, but they will not lord it over the sheep.
- The saints will submit to the elders' guidance.
- Deacons handle the physical affairs.
- The Lord's Supper (communion) is the center of the church's gathering and worship.
- Women are not in leadership, but they do teach other sisters how to be godly and to be homemakers.
- Women are silent when the Church is meeting together.
- Men are uncovered and women are covered at proper times.
- All believers are equally priests, thus, clergy-laity distinctions such as dress, titles, and special access or worship privileges for a select caste will be absent.
- A variety of men will exercise their responsibility, having liberty to use the different gifts in a church meeting to edify the body.
- Love will be shown to one another in the power of the Spirit.

It should now be clear that church government was not something God meant to be optional or flexible. For it is very important for the preserving and communication of truth and for the focusing of glory on the Lord Jesus Christ instead of on a man.

Section 14

The Gifts of the Church

The Disciple's Talents

Since the "gifts of the Spirit" are given to believers for the edification of the church, it is important to carefully examine this subject which has been much misunderstood. We will do this by searching the only source of truth on this subject, the Holy Scriptures. The following seven areas dealing with spiritual gifts will be presented in outline form:

A. Definition

B. Source

C. Scope

D. Purpose

E. Description of Gifts

F. Finding your Gift(s)

G. Scriptural Conclusions

A. Definition

A spiritual gift (Gk. *charisma*) is a spiritual enablement or talent given freely by God's grace. It must not be confused with natural ability or talent.

B. Source

God the Father – *"God hath dealt to every man...gifts."*
Rom. 12:3,6

God the Son – *"Christ...gave gifts unto men."*
Eph. 4:7,8

God the Spirit – *"There are diversities of gifts...given by the Spirit."* 1 Cor. 12:4,8

C. Scope

1. Every believer has at least one spiritual gift and perhaps more than one.
2. No believer has all the gifts and thus we are dependent upon one another for growth, Eph. 4.
3. Believers will each have **different** gifts, 1 Cor. 12:4.
4. Each believer can also have a **different** measure of the same gift, Rom. 12:3,6.
5. Each believer also has a **different** ministry for his gift, 1 Cor. 12:5.
6. Each believer also has a **different** activity in which his gift will operate, 1 Cor. 12:6.

Example – While several could have the same gift of teaching, one might have the ability to minister to children while another to adults. In addition, one person's gift might find its operation in a foreign country while another's only in his homeland.

D. Purpose

A believer is never gifted by God for his own needs or wants, but to build up and encourage his brothers and sisters. The Christian must be aware of wrong attitudes: pride – thinking yours is the only gift needed; false humility – "I'm no good and have nothing others need." Paul gives detailed controls in 1 Corinthians 12 - 14 so the purpose of the gifts will be fulfilled.

1 Corinthians 12
The Spirit's Choice – In deciding who gets what

vs. 15-16	No jealousy:	Why can't I be an eye?	***Contentment***
vs. 17-20	No clergy:	Is the whole body an eye?	***Involvement***
vs. 21-26	No independence:	I have no need of you	***Appreciation***

1 Corinthians 13
The Spirit's Oil - "Love" in seeking the welfare of others above yourself

1. Ability (gift) without love – ***I accomplish nothing***
2. Academics (knowledge) without love – ***I am nothing***
3. Actions (service) without love – ***I acquire nothing***

1 Corinthians 14
The Spirit's Control — His rules for an orderly church meeting that edifies

vs. 1-26 Understanding   Gifts must edify the whole church
vs. 27-40 Regulations   All things must be done in a godly order

E. Descriptions of Spiritual Gifts

There are two main categories for the gifts as God speaks of His church: the **foundation** and the **structure** or **building**, 1 Cor. 3:9-17. The foundation (gospel truth of Christ) is already laid and God used special gifts to break through the Jewish wall and to unite Jewish and Gentile believers in a new body in Christ. The wall is now down and the foundation is firmly set. Special gifts such as the apostles and mass miracles were used to do this. When one completes a foundation, the special tools (dynamite, bulldozers, etc.) are put away, and the structure that will rest on the foundation is built.

WARNING We, as Christians today, are told to be involved in the **building** of God's house. We are not told to lay the foundation; *"let every man take heed how he **buildeth** thereupon* [the foundation]." So let's not put God in a box and insist that He must use the exact gifts today on the 21st story (century) of the building structure that He required to lay the foundation in the 1st century.

At this point, we suggest you reread section 5 dealing with the blueprint for the church and the necessary transition it had to pass through from law to grace.

While the foundation gifts were mainly linked to the **apostles' experiences** and were given to break down the wall and to establish the one body, the building gifts are intended to help us continue, not in the apostles' experiences, but the **"apostles' doctrine"** – *"the word of his grace, which is able to build you up, and to give you an inheritance among all them which are sanctified,"* Acts 20:32.

The Gifts

Although to some degree, every Christian has a responsibility to be involved in many of these areas, the gifted will do it more effectively.

1 ***Apostle*** - 1 Cor. 12:28 – *A special messenger (sent one).*
- Those who had seen the Lord Jesus alive, Acts 1:21-23.
- Were involved in the foundation, Eph. 2:20.
- Emphasis on direct revelation from God as they were to finish writing the Bible, 2 Cor. 12 and Revelation.
- Had authority. There is no such thing as apostolic succession.

2 ***Prophet*** - 1 Cor. 12:28 – *A spokesman for God.*
- Were used in the foundation, Eph. 2:20.
- **Primary function:** reception of a direct revelation from God concerning a future event.
- **Secondary function:** speaking forth God's previously revealed Word, Acts 15:32.
- Results in edification, exhortation, and comfort.

3 ***Healings*** - 1 Cor. 12:28 – *To restore a sick body back to health.*
- God still heals today but not in the foundational way He did through the apostles, such as total community healings by Peter's shadow or by Paul's handkerchief.
- God did this for a unique reason: to bear witness to their new message, Heb. 2:4.
- Sick believers told to call for the elders of the church for prayer, James 5.

4 ***Miracles*** - 1 Cor. 12:10 – *Pertains usually to supernatural power over the process of nature.*

- Miracles such as changing water into wine, calming the sea, and raising the dead.
- God does miracles today but not in the consistent, foundational way of Christ and the apostles.

5 ***Tongues*** - Acts 2; 1 Cor. 14 – Gk. *glossa* – a language. *The supernatural ability to speak in a foreign language one has never learned.*

A careful study of Acts 2, 10, and 19 will show that tongues were greatly used in laying the foundation for the Jew and Gentile to be one in Christ.

Note: The gift of tongues is:

- not an evidence of salvation, 1 Cor. 12:30; Rom. 8:9
- not a proof of being filled with the Spirit, Eph. 5:18-21
- not an evidence of Spirit-baptism, 1 Cor. 12:13,30
- not given to every believer, 1 Cor. 12:4,10,30
- the same in Acts 2 as 1 Cor. 14
- a sign to the unbeliever, 1 Cor. 14:22
- completely useless to a church without an interpreter, 1 Cor. 14:28
- a gift that was designed to unify the early church, not divide it, Acts 10 - 11
- regulated by God with 5 rules in a church meeting, 1 Cor. 14
    a. the speaker **must** understand what he is saying, vs. 13-15
    b. there **must** be an interpreter for the congregation, v.28
    c. **only** two or three brothers may use that gift in a meeting, v.27
    d. each person in turn, i.e., **one at a time**, not together, v.27
    e. women are to keep **silent**, vs. 34,35

6 ***Interpreter*** - 1 Cor. 12:10 – *The supernatural ability to understand the foreign language (tongue) one has never learned and to translate it into the*

mother tongue for the congregation to understand.
This gift may or may not reside in the same person who has the gift of tongues, 1 Cor. 14:13.

7 ***Teacher*** - 1 Cor. 12:28 – *One who communicates effectively the divine truths of the Scripture so that others can understand and grow.*
Paul was a teacher, 1 Tim. 2:7.

8 ***Pastor*** - Eph. 4:11 – *One who has ability to caringly shepherd the flock.*
Note: this gift is not an office. A healthy church will have several pastors.

9 ***Evangelist*** - Eph. 4:11 – *A special ability to make the gospel message plain and clear, bringing others to know the Lord and Savior.*
He also equips the saints. Philip was an evangelist, Acts 8.

10 ***Exhortation*** - Rom. 12:8 – *To stir into action with Scripture so one will be encouraged in the right paths.*
Warns of danger. While teaching is for the mind, exhortation is primarily directed to the will and conscience. The stirring epistle to the Hebrews is an exhortation, 13:22.

11 ***Word of Wisdom*** - 1 Cor. 12:8 – *Applying biblical principles wisely to specific life situations.*
One has said that "knowledge" is knowing the facts, "wisdom" is knowing what to do with the facts. Stephen had this ability, Acts 6:10.

12 ***Word of Knowledge*** - 1 Cor. 12:8 – *The ability to know the will of God from Scripture for a difficult situation.*
James showed this ability at the Jerusalem council, Acts 15:13-21.

13 ***Faith*** - 1 Cor. 12:9 – *A special enablement to trust God for large or unusually difficult things.*
This encourages others in the power of God. Paul showed this in Acts 27:25.

14 ***Helps*** - 1 Cor. 12:28 – *To aid or support others.*
An undergirder or understudy. Aquila and Priscilla had this gift and used it greatly to help Paul, Rom. 16:3,4.

15 ***Governments*** - 1 Cor. 12:28 (also called administrations and ruling) – *To steer, organize, lead, and give direction in a spiritual and edifying way.*

This gift is often found in an elder and also in a deacon.

16 ***Ministry*** - Rom. 12:7 (also called service) – *Ability to forget self and to serve others.*

To render practical aid where needed. John Mark had this ability, Acts 13:5, and so did sister Phebe, Rom. 16:1.

17 ***Giving*** - Rom. 12:8 – *The divine enablement to give larger amounts with greater effectiveness than usual.*

18 ***Showing Mercy*** - Rom. 12:8 – *Ability to have compassion and to help those in sorrowful circumstances or in great need.*

Does not regard the condition of the object. Examples: the good Samaritan in Luke 10:37 and Dorcas in Acts 9:36.

19 ***Discernment of Spirits*** - 1 Cor. 12:10 – *A special ability to perceive the source behind any message or action.*

Peter showed this discernment with Ananias and Sapphira in Acts 5:3.

20 ***Hospitality*** - 1 Pet. 4:9,10 – *A form of serving that will involve the opening of one's home to care for, feed, and entertain God's people (as well as strangers) in a warm and edifying way.*

Aquila and Priscilla showed hospitality in Acts 18:3,26.

Quite a variety!

F. Finding Your Spiritual Gift

1. Know the gifts and relevant passages

Rom. 12:3-8
Emphasis on knowing your gift: **Involvement**

1 Cor. 12 - 14
Emphasis on understanding the differences: **Unity**

Eph. 4:7-16
Emphasis on the purpose: **Christ-like maturity**

1 Pet. 4:9-11
Emphasis on quality of use: **Accountability**

2. Think seriously: where do you seem to do better than usual by His grace? Beware of over-estimating yourself; Rom. 12:3, *"...not to think of himself more highly than he ought to think; but to think soberly, according as God hath dealt to every man the measure of faith* [gifts]*."*

3. Get involved in the service of the church. One will never know what he can do until he tries it. "A talent left unexercised will get dull." God gives the gift but we are responsible to use it. A Christian should pray for a servant's heart and for a burden for needs of the church, expecting to see God's guidance.

4. When you see an area of need that you feel unusually burdened about, follow that leading and try to meet it yourself. If the result of your action is inner satisfaction and the blessing of others, this should be investigated.

5. The elders of the local church should see to it that time, opportunity, and guidance are provided for those to serve while searching.

6. Attitude of honesty: neither pride nor false humility. Distinguish between the blessing that comes to others from exercise of gift and gracious remarks meant to encourage us, or mere flattery.

7. Seek the guidance of older believers. It is rare for one to have a gift that others don't see.

8. Have patience. Proverbs 18:16 reminds us that *"A man's gift maketh room for him."* It is not necessary to push a door open. God will open it if it's according to His will.

9. *"Neglect not the gift that is in thee...Stir up the gift of God, which is in thee,"* 1 Tim. 4:14; 2 Tim. 1:6.

WARNING A gifted person will feel more burdened in the area in which he is gifted. Example: Evangelist – souls, Teacher – doctrine, Pastors – growth, Showing mercy – compassion, Giving – financial needs, Governments – correct organization, etc. **Understand, these differences are natural**. Rather than criticizing others for not being burdened or as involved in an area as you are, respect the differences and do your work to the best of your ability while letting them follow their leading from God. Don't squeeze everyone into the mold of your gift and burden.

G. Concluding Thoughts

- It is sinful to ignore one's spiritual gift and the exercise of it, Luke 19:11-27. Also, it's wrong to attempt to exercise a gift we don't have and thereby to exclude another brother or sister.

- Scriptures **do not** teach: one-man ministry (immature Christians follow a man), gifts given by men, exaltation of gifted men by flattering titles such as "reverend," "pastor," "rabbi," etc. Job 32:21 – *"Let me not, I pray you, accept any man's person, neither let me give flattering titles unto man."*

- Gifts are never the bottom line. They are a means to an end. **The gifts of the Spirit** are meant to convey the **truth of the Spirit** (the Word) which is meant to produce the **fruit of the Spirit.** To be like Christ, ***this is the bottom line.***

- Never justify using your gift by a method which disobeys the written Word or is not glorifying to the Lord. Despite the results, obedience is more important to God. *"...Yet is he not crowned, except he strive lawfully,"* 2 Tim. 2:5.

Section 15

THE FELLOWSHIP OF THE CHURCH:

Maintaining and Solving Interpersonal Relationships

The Disciple's Love

Although it is a privilege to be part of a sports team, much responsibility is required to make the team perform smoothly. God's assembly calls for the same participation. All players on the team make up one team or body. When one does well, all benefit from it. However, when one makes a mistake, it also affects all the members. No one man is an island unto himself. This is how 1 Corinthians 12:26 describes the local church at Corinth who was the body of Christ: *"And whether one member suffer,* ***all*** *the members suffer with it; or one member be honoured,* ***all*** *the members rejoice with it."*

The above description of people working together is what the Bible calls "fellowship." Fellowship is one of the four basics, found in Acts 2:42, that Christians need. The following chart of the basic four activities of the assembly may be helpful in seeing how fellowship fits into God's plan.

Acts 2:42

MEETING	FOCUS	RESULT
Teaching	***Truth***	*Learning*
*** Fellowship ***	**** Other Believers ****	** Comfort **
Breaking of Bread	***Lord Jesus***	*Worship*
Prayer	***Needs***	*Answered Prayer*

Christian fellowship is a continuation of the common life of Jesus and His disciples through the Holy Spirit. Since the world generally turns its back on the faithful Christian, it is of utmost importance that a Christian find fellowship within the body, a church home where disciples meet together under the Lord Jesus.

The Greek word for fellowship is *koinonia* and is translated in the KJV the following ways:

Fellowship	Contribute	Partakers
Communion	Communicated	Partner
Distributing	Companion	

Think of two fellows in a ship rowing the same way to understand *fellow ship*. When one is received into God's local church, there is much privilege as well as much responsibility involved in enjoying fellowship. A believer who is coming into a church fellowship should be sharing a common belief in the Lord Jesus, in His gospel, and in His Word (though they might not understand it all yet). They should be willing to be part of the team, submitting to the authority of the elders. **This should be understood from the beginning.** If they are not willing to believe the common faith and to submit to authority, then how can they really be part of the church fellowship? For then, instead of "fellowship," you have schisms and divisions which are not of God.

The term "one another" (Gk. *allelon*) expresses the privileges and responsibilities of fellowship. It involves Christ-like relationships with people, i.e., fellow believers. This word is used 100 times in the N.T. in at least 30 different ways as follows:

Have peace ***one*** *with* ***another***	Mark 9:50
Wash ***one another's*** *feet*	John 13:14
Love ***one another***	John 13:34
Members ***one*** *of* ***another***	Rom. 12:5
In honour preferring ***one another***	Rom. 12:10
Same mind ***one*** *toward* ***another***	Rom. 12:16

Not to judge ***one another***	Rom. 14:13
Edify ***one another***	Rom. 14:19
Receive ***one another***	Rom 15:7
Admonish [counsel] ***one another***	Rom. 15:14
Greet ***one another***	Rom. 16:16
Tarry ***one*** *for* ***another***	1 Cor. 11:33
Have care ***one*** *for* ***another***	1 Cor. 12:25
Serve ***one another***	Gal. 5:13
Bear ***one another's*** *burdens*	Gal. 6:2
Forbearing ***one another***	Eph. 4:2
Be kind ***one*** *to* ***another***	Eph. 4:32
Forgiving ***one another*** *(diff. Gk word)*	Eph. 4:32
Speaking Psalms to yourselves [**one another**]	Eph. 5:19
*Submitting...***one** *to* ***another***	Eph. 5:21
Each *esteem* ***other*** *better*	Phil. 2:3
Lie not ***one*** *to* ***another***	Col. 3:9
Comfort yourselves ***together***	1 Thess. 5:11
Exhort ***one another***	Heb. 3:13
Consider ***one another***	Heb. 10:24
Speak not evil ***one*** *of* ***another***	James 4:11
Grudge not ***one*** *against* ***another***	James 5:9
Confess your faults ***one*** *to* ***another***	James 5:16
Pray ***one*** *for* ***another***	James 5:16
Use hospitality ***one*** *toward* ***another***	1 Pet. 4:9
Fellowship ***one*** *with* ***another***	1 Jn. 1:7
Beloved, let us love ***one another***	1 Jn. 4:7

Fellowshipping in Christian love means one will be concerned about the other person as well as himself. A believer does not represent Christ only in the church meeting but everywhere, seven days a week, twenty-four hours a day. Love is to be the distinguishing mark of a Christian – the difference that will convince the world we are the Lord's disciples.

Solving Interpersonal Problems

The special fellowship of Christian love and care must be zealously worked at to be maintained for His glory. One will find that because of human personality, maintaining Christian fellowship in love will call for much forgiving and forbearing. The Word of God gives implicit instructions on how to settle interpersonal problems among Christians.

1. **Submission**

   This is the attitude of being willing to stay under or give in to another. It is the opposite of pride (to lift up and go above the other person). *"Yea, all of you be subject one to another, and be clothed with **humility**: for God resisteth the **proud**, and giveth grace to the humble,"* 1 Pet. 5:5.

   Remember, the attitude of pride (to lift up over another) is Satanic, Isa. 14:14, *"I will ascend."* Prov. 13:10 – "***Only by pride cometh contention.***" But, the attitude of humility (to come down) is Christ-like, Phil. 2:8, *"He humbled himself, and became obedient."*

2. **Hiding it**

   You may choose in love to cover (hide) a wrong done to you. In other words, for the sake of peace and unity you choose to endure it, to keep it to yourself instead of making an issue out of it. *"And above all things have fervent charity* [love] *among yourselves: for charity shall cover the multitude of sins,"* 1 Pet. 4:8.

3. **Confrontation. *Step #1 in restoring broken fellowship***

   If it is a situation in which you feel the wrong must be dealt with, then you have the right to confront the individual. You are to go to the person *alone* in the spirit of meekness with the goal of trying to settle it, Gal. 6:1. **Most problems could be settled right here if we would go to the person instead of telling others.** *"Moreover if thy brother shall trespass against thee, go and tell him his fault between thee and him alone: if he shall hear thee, thou hast gained thy brother,"* Matt. 18:15.

4. Forgiveness

If you have confronted the person and the person repents, you are to forgive him. That means the matter is closed and should never be brought up again to anyone. Even if he repeats the offense seven times in one day and still repents each time, you are to keep forgiving. *"If thy brother trespass against thee, rebuke him; and if he* ***repent, forgive him.*** *And if he trespass against thee seven times in a day, and seven times in a day turn again to thee, saying, I repent; thou shalt forgive him,"* Luke 17:3,4.

However, if he is wrong and does not repent, then there can't really be any true reconciliation or forgiveness. For it takes two to reconcile. In such a case, the Lord Jesus taught that another step is now necessary to heal the problem and to restore real fellowship. Glossing over it and hoping it will go away is not the answer.

5. Bring in Witnesses. *Step #2 in restoring broken fellowship*

Now (if the person remains unrepentant) you are to bring into the problem one or two witnesses to try to solve it. *"But if he will not hear thee, then take with thee one or two more, that in the mouth of two or three witnesses every word may be established,"* Matt. 18:16.

Preferably, these witnesses are ones who have observed the problem and so can make an intelligent judgment. If this can't be done, then the witnesses will have to hear the stories from both sides so they can give witness to the words said and to the problem. The witnesses then make a judgment. If the witnesses agree with the other person's side, then the case is closed and you must accept the verdict. If the witnesses agree with your side and the other person then repents, you are to forgive him and the case is closed.

However, if the person is declared wrong by the witnesses and still won't repent, you have one final step left to try to restore fellowship.

5. **Tell it to the Church. *Final step to restore fellowship***

   You must now take the unrepentant person and the problem to the whole local assembly (through the eldership). *"And if he shall neglect to hear them, tell it unto the church,"* Matt. 18:17.

   The church has God-given authority to make a judgment on the case. **Their decision is binding** (18:18), and you must submit to it. There is no higher court of appeal – this is God's supreme court on earth. You are not to take the matter into your own hands, nor are you to go to an unsaved court of the world, 1 Cor. 6. Christ Himself will be in the midst of the praying assembly to give it wisdom to solve the dispute. Heaven itself will sanction the church's final decision.

   If the church agrees with you, perhaps this will break the person and they will repent and then fellowship is fully restored. But, if the person still won't repent, ***it is at this point that fellowship is to be completely broken.*** The person is to be treated as an unsaved person – *"...but if he neglect* ***to hear the church,*** *let him be unto thee as an heathen man and a publican,"* Matt. 18:17.

Maintaining Christian fellowship is a tall order in today's world, but you can do it because: Christ lives for you as an intercessor, the Holy Spirit lives in you to empower you, and God's church is the channel through which the body works with its various gifts to build you up in love.

WARNING	To ignore the church and its fellowship is to ignore God's way for Christian living.

In maintaining sweet fellowship, it is also true that younger Christians must be shown patience and be given room for growth in many areas, just as we all needed and still need. Remember, the church is not for perfect saints but *"for the* ***perfecting*** [maturing] *of the saints,"* Eph. 4:12. However, lack of growth is not a valid excuse to disobey a clear command of the Lord. If you don't understand the logic of a command, just yield and obey it by faith anyway – God can give understanding later, Phil. 3:15,16. Be like Abraham who *"by faith...obeyed...not knowing,"* Heb. 11:8.

Let's move on to section 16 to see how understanding Christian liberty or freedom is an important area in maintaining the unity of Christian fellowship.

Section 16

Christian Liberty and Freedom

The Disciple's Convictions

There are many truths and commands in the Scripture that are clear issues. They are not open to debate, they are to be obeyed. However, due to different cultures and heritages, some Christians will have a more difficult time in understanding their freedom in Christ than others. Some will have ***weak*** consciences, sincerely believing that God still requires certain rules to be performed (which have passed away with the Old Covenant). Others will be ***strong*** in the faith, realizing that certain things don't matter anymore as we are freed from them through the reality of Jesus Christ. The question is, how should the strong and weak react to each other when they have different convictions?

There are also many areas where specific instruction is not given by God. In this case there is liberty for believers to do the right thing in different ways. The unique circumstances of each situation might dictate a different approach. What is right for one might be wrong for another. The question should then be asked, which way will bring the most glory to God?

The church is not under Jewish law with its hundreds of ordinances that controlled their many actions. The church is not to be compared to or managed like a military camp with rules and regulations for every step. It must be remembered that sometimes there can be two or more ways of doing something right. Thus, close communion with the Lord is necessary to discern His will rather than proceeding by a list of rules. There must be liberty within the church for such things as: time schedules, cultural habits, dress styles, arrangement of meetings, music, foods one eats, drink (wine) one drinks, special days of celebrations, and other areas.

Regarding these "liberty areas" the Scriptures teach three main principles for maintaining the unity of the faith as found in Romans 14 and 1 Corinthians 8 - 10.

1. "Let every man be fully persuaded in his own mind." Rom. 14:5

We must allow a fellow believer to arrive at convictions with his own mind. Do not try to force your mind on him to fit him into your mold. This can be cultic mind oppression. Thus, we are to receive each other without arguing, though our convictions may be different, because the Lord has seen fit to receive us.

2. Not stumbling your brother is the more important issue.

Do not look at someone as being "less spiritual" because his convictions are different. The main issue here isn't how right we are. The higher issue is that our brother needs love and so we should not cause him to stumble, Rom. 14:13. You see, if you continue to do your conviction your way in front of your brother and therefore, by your example, he gains the boldness to violate the different conviction he held, you have actually caused him to go against his personal faith and therefore to sin against Christ. For though your belief might have been "more Scriptural," your action was not, Rom. 14:23; 1 Cor. 8:9-13.

We must remember, not only are we to do what's right between us and God, but our actions must appear right in the eyes of our fellow man. They can't see God but they can see our actions. 2 Corinthians 8:21 states: *"Providing for honest things, not only* ***in the sight of the Lord****, but also in the* ***sight of men****."*

There are two groups of people our lifestyle must not stumble or offend:

1. The unsaved world - with its different cultures (Jew and Gentile), 1 Cor. 9.

2. The church of God - There are older Christians with godly customs as well as younger ones watching and learning, 1 Cor. 10:32.

3. God looks at the attitude of the heart above the action.

Some convictions can be actually "more right" in the eyes of God, but if, because of a weak conscience, you are convicted that it is wrong, then God still respects the attitude that you hold because you sincerely believe it will offend Him. Thus, God is still glorified by the attitude of your heart, Rom. 14:4-9.

Therefore, even if something might be Scripturally right in the eyes of God, but your weak conscience believes it wrong, it is indeed sin for you if you do it, 1 Cor. 8:7; Rom. 14:20-23. It might be perfectly right for someone else to do it, but God would count you as sinning because He saw the attitude of your heart. You did not care enough for Him to stay true to what you believed was right in His eyes. This is why if you cause your brother to do a right thing which he doesn't believe is right, you and he are both wrong. Think about it!

The Uniqueness of Christian Love

God, who operates with the Christian on the principle of love and grace, wants His children to operate with each other the same way. One of the greatest commandments to the church is, *"Beloved let us love one another: for love is of God,"* 1 Jn. 4:7. This, too, is assembly truth and is part of the apostles' doctrine.

In our dark world, much is said, sung, and preached about love. To different people it may mean anything from lustful desires to caring for someone's material needs. However, the true meaning of Christian love is made clear in this area of Christian liberty. God teaches a "higher way" than just doing something because you know you have liberty and because it doesn't bother God. The "higher way" is that in all our actions we consider our brother above ourselves.

In this world we all have certain human rights, but in the Christian world you have an extra right: the option of giving up your rights to help others grow. As 1 Corinthians 8:9 says, *"But take heed lest by any means this liberty of yours becomes a stumblingblock to them that are weak."* Do not use your liberty as a mask to do your own thing, but by love serve one another, Gal. 5:13. Yes, if something truly offends your brother, give it up in love, not for your sake but for his. *"Conscience, I say, not thine own, but of the other,"* 1 Cor. 10:29.

Though all things are lawful to the strong Christian, all things are not expedient nor will all things build others up, 1 Cor. 10:23. You might have the liberty to eat certain meats, drink wine, wear certain clothes, etc., but the apostle's word in regard to actions that mislead, offend or stumble any brother, was:

"Wherefore, if meat make my brother to offend,
I will eat no flesh while the world standeth," 1 Cor. 8:13.

This is truly self-sacrificial and can be called love, for *"love...seeks not her own,"* 1 Cor. 13:5.

On these open areas, respect another's convictions even though they're different from yours. Out of gratitude, take the attitude of giving latitude.

Remember again, we are not wedded to a religious military system or to a cult, but to a living Savior, the loving Lord, Rom. 7:4-6. Ask yourself when faced with these decisions: *What would Jesus do?*

1 Cor. 10:31
"Whether therefore ye eat, or drink,
or whatsoever ye do, do all to the glory of God."

How often do we destroy a fellow brother with our convictions?

Destroy not him with thy meat, for whom Christ died...
For meat destroy not the work of God." Rom. 14:15,20

Section 17

FINANCIAL GIVING:
A Responsibility in Love

The Disciple's Money

This is an important subject and one addressed by God. However, it is also misunderstood and abused by many. So, let's look at the New Testament for instructions on the way the church is to give money to the Lord.

Obviously, the church lives in a material world and must use money to operate. The living God promised to supply the church's needs, Phil. 4:19, and does so through His body. Remember, Ephesians 4:16 says that the body, through its Christ-given gifts, was designed to be self supporting, *"the edifying of itself in love."* ***One of the gifts is giving***, Rom. 12. That's why you will never find the apostle or any other servant appealing to the unsaved for money to do God's work. The living Lord is powerful enough to support His own work through His body alone. Giving to the work of the Lord is a privilege given only to the church of God. Think about the following Bible statements:

Matt. 10:8	*"...freely ye have received,* ***freely*** *give."*
2 Cor. 11:7	*"I have preached to you the gospel of God* ***freely****."*
Phil. 4:6	*"Let your requests be made known unto God."*
Phil. 4:19	*"But my God shall supply all your need."*
3 John 7	*"Because that for his name's sake they went forth,* ***taking nothing*** *of the Gentiles."*

Neither will one find any pressure tactics used to get the Christian's money. In 2 Corinthians 8 and 9 we read of Christians who were "willing of themselves" to give to other needy saints, having given themselves to God first. Paul then encouraged them to keep their voluntary promise. Notice in 1 Corinthians 16:1,2 that the Christians were to lay up in advance what each had determined to give, so when Paul arrived, there would be no need for an offering or collection. Quite unlike today.

The New Testament knows nothing of:

a) churches appealing for money to either the unsaved or the saved
b) fund raising projects
c) pledges
d) faith promises
e) missionaries "getting up their support" (deputation)
f) "free give-aways" if you send in a gift

These things are found nowhere in Scripture. Indeed, the apostles carried out an extensive outreach program lasting for years and covering thousands of miles without a single mention of personal financial need.

It is also true that a servant of the Lord who gives up secular employment, either full or part time, has a God-given right to be financially helped by God's church. *"For it is written in the law of Moses, Thou shalt not muzzle the mouth of the ox that treadeth out the corn...if we have sown unto you spiritual things, is it a great thing if we shall reap your carnal things?"* 1 Cor. 9:9,11. But blessed is that man or woman who simply claims the promises of the living Lord by faith, and for support looks to God alone who is able to use the body of Christ in a marvelous way.

Looking to God to minister through His church rather than trusting the church to minister for God by a stipulated salary, keeps one daily dependent upon the promises of God and free from human strings. As Philippians 4:6 says, *"Let your requests be **made known**"* – but unto whom? Answer – ***"unto God."*** Then verse 19 promises: *"But my God shall supply all your need according to his riches in glory by Christ Jesus."*

Giving, New Testament Style: *Stewardship*

In the Old Testament, we see that tithing (giving 10% of one's goods) was mandatory. In addition, there were freewill offerings above that tithe to the Lord. Tithing was just the beginning. *"And all the tithe of the land, whether of the seed of the land, or of the fruit of the tree, is the LORD'S...the tenth shall be holy unto the LORD,"* Lev. 27:30,32. However, in the New Covenant, ***the church is never once commanded to tithe.*** The only time you will ever read about tithing in the N.T. epistles is in Hebrews 7 where we are told it is *"according to the law,"* vs. 5.

Pre-Law	Abraham	Tithing	Gen. 14:20
O.T. Law	Israel	Tithing	Lev. 27; Num. 18
N.T. Grace	The Church	Never mentioned	————

In the N.T., Christians are called "stewards." *"Moreover it is required in stewards, that a man be found faithful,"* 1 Cor. 4:2. A steward is one who has been entrusted with the management of property, finances, truth, etc. – things not his own. Everything the believer possesses has been given to him from God and we are responsible to use all of it for His glory. The biblical concept of stewardship isn't that 90% percent is ours and 10% is God's, *but that all our possessions are God's.*

God does want His children to use their finances for Him, but motivated by love which proves that we are responsible stewards. While it is not wrong for a Christian to tithe if that's what he individually decides before the Lord, it is not a mandatory amount God requires for the church.

There are 3 types of givers:

The Rock – *to get anything out of it you must hammer it and the sparks fly*

The Sponge – *the more pressure you squeeze with, the more comes out*

The Rose – *its naturally sweet fragrance is given freely*

Upon studying this new way of giving for the church in the New Testament, the following are some principles. 2 Corinthians 8 and 9 are the main chapters dealing with New Testament giving.

New Testament Giving Principles

1 **Sacrificial giving.** Giving even though you may be deprived of things, 2 Cor. 8:2. *"To communicate* [give] *forget not: for with such sacrifices God is well pleased,"* Heb. 13:16.

2 **Freewill.** To be willing of yourself. No emotional appeals or guilt to coerce you to give. *"They were willing of themselves,"* 2 Cor. 8:3,12.

3 **Motive is love.** The motive for giving is love because of the grace of Christ who became poor to make us rich. *"For ye know the grace of our Lord Jesus Christ,"* 2 Cor. 8:9.

4 **Proportionate giving.** No set amount or tithe is required, but you decide how much to give according to how God has individually prospered you. *"Let every one of you lay by him in store, as God hath prospered him...Every man according to his ability, determined to send relief unto the brethren,"* 1 Cor. 16:2; Acts 11:29. Every Christian will therefore give differently.

5 **Equality for all.** A good guideline to determine how much to give and to whom, is that God teaches there should be an equality among Christians. One should not be lacking necessities while another has abundance. *"That there may be an equality,"* 2 Cor. 8:13-15.

6 **Individual Decision.** It is a matter of a personal choice between you and God what you give. There is no law telling you how much it is necessary to give, but a heart commitment is to motivate you. *"Every man according as he purposeth in his heart, so let him give; not grudgingly, or of necessity,"* 2 Cor. 9:7.

7 **Cheerful giving.** Not because you have to but because you want to. *"For God loveth a cheerful giver,"* 2 Cor. 9:7.

8 **Advance Planning.** You are to plan and lay up in advance what

you determine to give. Not a hyper-emotional, haphazard, or spasmodic giving. *"Let every one of you lay by him in store...that there be no gatherings* [collections] *when I come,"* 1 Cor. 16:2.

9 **You give; God gives back.** As you give, God will see to it that you have your needs met, and He will supply extra so you can continue giving. *"But this I say, He which soweth sparingly shall reap also sparingly; and he which soweth bountifully shall reap also bountifully...And God is able to make all grace abound toward you; that ye, always having all sufficiency in all things, may abound to every good work,"* 2 Cor. 9:6,8. This is the circle of love.

10 **Giving is not losing but gaining.** You really aren't giving your wealth away but investing it, for the Lord will reward you with heavenly treasure. *"Lay up for yourselves treasures in heaven,"* Matt. 6:20. Jim Elliot, a martyred missionary to the Auca Indians, said: *"He is no fool who gives what he cannot keep, to gain what he cannot lose."*

11 **Giving causes God to receive praise.** The recipient, in being helped, will give glory to God. *"This service not only supplieth the want of the saints, but is abundant also by many thanksgivings unto God,"* 2 Cor. 9:12.

12 **Give to a Scriptural cause.** Supporting something wrong is not giving to the Lord, even though the concern might be religious. *"If any man teach otherwise, and consent not to wholesome words, even the words of our Lord Jesus Christ...from such withdraw thyself,"* 1 Tim. 6:3,5.

13 **Give secretly.** Do not let anyone know what you are giving. Having your name etched on crystal panes or chapel bricks of a ministry to which you donated, or posting a certificate in your office showing how much you gave to a ministry, is against the teaching of our Lord. Your only reward for that gift will be the recognition you get from men down here. *"Take heed that ye do not your alms before men, to be seen of them: otherwise ye have no reward of your Father which is in heaven...that thine alms may be in secret,"* Matt. 6:1,4.

14 **Pay off your debts.** It would be an unwise testimony to give

much to the Lord when you owe debts to man. *"Owe no man anything, but to love one another,"* Rom. 13:8.

15 **Amount left, not amount given, is what counts.** In God's calculation the value of a gift is not measured by the quantity, but by what remains in the giver's possession. *"This poor widow hath cast more in, than all they which have cast into the treasury: For all they did cast in of their abundance; but she of her want did cast in all that she had, even all her living,"* Mark 12:43,44.

In summary, God loves a cheerful giver, and we are to be responsible stewards with what God has entrusted to us.

Section 18

THE CHURCH'S FUTURE

The Disciple's Vision

Although we have looked at many instructions from the Bible about the church on earth, it is not God's plan to leave His church down here forever. He has glorious plans for the future of His church. We will consider these plans under five headings.

1. Ambassadors Come Home
2. The Church Goes Extra Terrestrial
3. The Judgment Seat
4. The Marriage and Reception
5. Reigning with the King

1. Ambassadors Come Home

An ambassador is an appointed representative of his own country who lives in another country. 2 Corinthians 5:20 calls Christians *"ambassadors for Christ."* Since Christ, our Head, is in heaven, we, the body, represent Him on earth with the gospel message of reconciliation. There are some enlightening truths connected with being an ambassador:

a. Ambassadors are not citizens of the country in which they serve but are citizens of their home country. Christians are not of this world but their citizenship is in heaven.

b. Ambassadors represent the wishes of their home country. As Christians we are not to please ourselves but Him who called us.

c. Ambassadors have no vote of power in the country they are assigned to. They do not try to change the government or system of their assigned country. Christians are never commanded to reform Satan's world system through politics, social reform, etc. They are, however, to represent the message of the gospel which does transform an individual.

d. Ambassadors conduct themselves in a way that will speak well of their homeland's president. They try not to do anything that would make their home country look bad. Christians are to live like Christ, so the world will see the reality of Him.

e. Ambassadors sometimes endure persecution from the foreign country when their policies conflict. Christians who live godly lives, since they are in an enemy country, will suffer persecution for the Lord Jesus Christ.

f. When war is declared, ambassadors are immediately called home. During the loosing of the seven seals, God wages war on planet earth. But God will first call the church home (rapture), *"not appointed to wrath, but to obtain salvation by our Lord Jesus Christ,"* 1 Thess. 5:9.

2. The Church Goes Extra Terrestrial

Someday, at the appointed time, the trumpet will blow and the Lord Jesus will leave the throne in heaven and descend to the air. His purpose will be to gather His church to Himself in heaven. Whether dead or alive, at that split-second, every true Christian will have his body transformed into a heavenly body. The church's mission as ambassadors will be finished as war is declared on the earth and judgment day will have arrived.

This meeting in the air, 1 Thess. 4:13-18; 1 Cor. 15:51-58, is sometimes called the "rapture." Rapture means to be caught up and at this future event every believer will be ***"caught up** together...to meet the Lord in the air."* This is a separate event from the revelation of Jesus Christ when He comes the second time to earth and actually touches down on the Mount of Olives, Matt. 24; Zech. 14:3,4.

3. The Judgment Seat

In God's program immediately following the rapture is "the judgment seat of Christ." This judgment is for Christians only, and it has nothing to do with getting into heaven or hell, for at this point the Christian is already in heaven because of grace. This is a judgment on the life of the Christian. The believer is told in 2 Corinthians 5:10: *"For we must all appear before the judgment seat of Christ; that every one may receive the things done in his body, according to that he hath done, whether it be good or bad."*

This is the time when good works do count. Good works do not cancel out sins nor do they merit heaven, but they do earn bonuses or rewards in heaven. This is the time when God will review your Christian life and will reward you or withhold rewards according to your performance.

WARNING There is **equality** in the way we get into heaven: *"For ye are all the children of God by faith in Christ Jesus,"* Gal. 3:26. However, there will be **inequality** in our positions and rewards in heaven because of different performances for the Lord.

Following is a brief outline to help us understand the judgment seat of Christ.

A. Input equals Output

The rewards you receive depend upon the amount of good works you did for God. Where you did "bad works," rewards will be lost. *"If any man's **work** abide...he shall receive a reward. If any man's **work** shall be burned, he shall suffer loss: but he himself shall be saved,"* 1 Cor. 3:14,15.

B. Accountable for only Yourself

One will not have to stand before God and answer for his neighbor's life, but we will give a full account of our own actions to the living God. *"But why dost thou judge thy brother?...for we shall all stand before the judgment seat of Christ...So then every one of us shall give* ***account of himself*** *to God,"* Rom. 14:10,12.

C. This is your Life

God, who knows all things, will play back the video of your Christian life. 1 Corinthians 3:13 teaches that these four things will happen:

1. Life made manifest	*made known*
2. Life declared	*published*
3. Life revealed	*uncovered*
4. Life tried	*tested*

D. Two areas of Judgment

1. Things done in the body, good or bad – *"...that every one may receive the things done in his body, according to that he hath done, whether it be good or bad,"* 2 Cor. 5:10.

2. Counsels (motives) of the heart – *"Until the Lord come...and will make manifest the counsels of the hearts,"* 1 Cor. 4:5.

E. Areas of Rewards

Many think that winning souls is the only thing rewarded. However, upon studying the N.T. one will find a large list of actions that God cares about and will reward.

- ***Working in God's Church***
- ***Enduring Persecution***
- ***Loving Enemies***
- ***Kindness to God's Saints***
- ***Faith***
- ***Separating from False Doctrine***
- ***Submitting to Authority***
- ***Soul Winning - Witnessing***
- ***Financial Giving***
- ***Good Shepherding by Elders***
- ***Holy Living***
- ***Obeying God's Word***

F. Types of Rewards

1. Control	*"ruler over many things"*	Matt. 25
2. Clothing	*"fine linen"*	Rev. 19:7,8
3. Crowns	*"there is laid up for me a crown"*	2 Tim. 4:8

Although a true Christian cannot lose God's salvation, he can lose rewards. Therefore, it pays to:

Suffer now - Rejoice later!

4. The Marriage and the Reception

Once the judgment seat of Christ has taken place, the church is now made ready as the wife. She is clothed in fine white linen which are her righteous acts. This is known as *"the marriage of the Lamb."* The church will be formally united with her Lord and Savior, Jesus Christ. Then follows the great celebration at the reception known as *"the marriage supper of the Lamb,"* Rev. 19:7-9.

5. Reigning with the King

Now the Lord Jesus is ready to be revealed from heaven in dazzling splendor. The seven years of tribulation are ended and Christ is united with His wife. The rebelling world will be crushed and the kingdom of God on earth will now be established. The good news for the church is that, as His wife, we will be coming back with Him to share in reigning over the world. *"And hast made us unto our God kings and priests: and **we shall reign on the earth,**"* Rev. 5:10.

The church will have reached its ultimate goal for which God has been training it all along – reigning over the new world. When the Lord Jesus descends from heaven, behind Him will be not only the angels, but also the saints (church included) of God.

- *"...the coming of our Lord Jesus Christ with all His saints."*
- *"Behold, the Lord cometh with ten thousands of His saints."*
- *"And the Lord my God shall come, and all the saints with thee."*
  1 Thess. 3:13; Jude 14; Zech. 14:5

Jesus Christ will be revealed from heaven as *"King of kings and Lord of lords."* After a thousand-year kingdom on earth, He will then set up a new heaven and new earth in which there will be no more tears, death, sorrow, crying, or pain. All things will be new, Rev. 20, 21, and *"they* [church included] *shall reign forever and ever,"* Rev. 22:5.

Thus, we have the history of the church by grace alone:

from sinful rebels deserving hell to forgiven Christians –

from forgiven Christians to obedient children and ambassadors on earth –

from ambassadors on earth to the wife of the Son in heaven –

from the wife of the Son in heaven to a kingdom of priests reigning in paradise forever.

"Thanks be unto God for His unspeakable gift."

2 Cor. 9:15

Concluding Thoughts

The few years we spend on this earth are the decisive years for the saved. These earthly years determine one's position for all the future in the eternal kingdom. Yes, our never-ending future is determined by our approximately 50 to 70 years now. The following is an illustration:

The earth icon represents the short time of our existence here on the earth in comparison with our eternal existence represented by the circles. Each dot represents a billion years. However, it is the globe that is most important for it determines the remainder forever.

WARNING Since 50-70 years determine billions of years, *"redeem the time,"* for there is coming that sudden moment when your eternal position in the kingdom of God will become fixed and unchangeable.

My prayer and desire is that upon studying the Scriptural truth presented in this discipleship manual concerning *"Christ and the Church,"* you will see the high value God puts on His church for which Christ shed His blood. The Lord Jesus Christ is totally committed to the church, for He died for it and lives for it. I trust that your answer to the question asked at the beginning of this study manual from 1 Corinthians 11:22, ***"Despise ye the church of God?"*** is a resounding "no". Blessed is the man or woman who builds his or her life around Christ – and His church.

The Big Picture:

Why God does things in unusual ways

Many things connected with the church may be hard to understand at times. Therefore, always keep the big picture in focus. The eternal kingdom is the final goal where we will reign over creation with Him. As 1 Corinthians 6:2,3 asks:

> *"Do ye not know that the saints shall judge the world?"*
>
> *"Know ye not that we shall judge angels?"*

You see, the church age is simply ***training for reigning***. God is simply proving us with various commandments to see if we will obey His Word in all areas. Thus, He will know in what position He can use us in the eternal state.

We see this lesson brought out in the O.T. when the children of Israel were journeying to their promised land. At times, rather than Sovereignly solving the problem or meeting their need, God attached ordinances or commandments to the situation that were seemingly unnecessary. When the waters were bitter at Marah, God could have made them sweet instantly, but instead He gave an order that a tree must be cast into the water. Why this extra baggage? The Bible says it was to prove (test) them to see if they would keep His future ordinances and statutes, Ex. 15:25,26.

Another example is in Exodus 16, when the children of Israel were hungry and God provided manna from heaven. God could have just spoken the word and there could have been a bagel on every bush. Instead, He gave them the extra baggage of rules on how to obtain it, such as amounts gathered, times to gather, and penalties if violated. Why? God gives His reason in Exodus 16:4, *"That I may prove* [test] *them, whether they will walk in my law, or no."*

Yes, God takes pains to do things in strange manners so that we will realize that we just don't live by the material but *"to humble thee, and to **prove** thee, to know what was in thine heart, whether thou wouldest **keep his commandments**, or no...That he might make thee know that man doth not live by bread only, but by **every word** that proceedeth out of the mouth of the LORD doth man live...That he might prove* [test] *thee, to do thee good at thy **latter end**,"* Deut. 8:2,3,16.

So, dear saint of God and disciple of the Lord Jesus, don't be surprised if you can't make sense out of all the commands for the church. Things such as the different roles for men and women, head-covering, church government, etc., what we might consider "excess baggage", is all part of the plan to test and train us in obedience to His every Word for that greater day of reigning with Christ. Remember, *"That the **trial*** [test] *of your faith, being much more precious than of gold that perisheth, though it be tried with fire, might be found unto praise and honour and glory **at the appearing of Jesus Christ**,"* 1 Pet. 1:7.

The Key to Revival

There is much talk about renewal and revival. The word revived means – "a renewed interest in the things of God after neglecting them." Did you know that a revival doesn't begin with the unsaved world but with the people of God? When the house of God (church) wakes up to the things of God, then the Holy Spirit can work mightily through God's power tool in this world, His church. See 2 Chronicles 7:14 and 1 Peter 4:17.

Any real revival among the people of God will involve hearts turning to the written word and obeying it no matter what the cost. We see this during the revival in King Hezekiah's day in 2 Chronicles 29 - 31. The key was not just a knowledge of the written word but **action**. This is true repentance. The term "Bible-believing Christian" is a popular label today. However, Bible action and obedience is the real test. These are some ingredients of the ***true*** revival during Hezekiah's day:

*"We have **cleansed** all the house of the Lord."* 2 Chron. 29:18

*"So the service of the house of the Lord was set in **order**."* 2 Chron. 29:35

*"...as it was **written**."* 2 Chron. 30:5

*"...one heart...to do...the **word** of the Lord."* 2 Chron. 30:12

*"...brake the images in pieces, and cut down the groves...until they had **utterly** destroyed them all."* 2 Chron. 31:1

*"...as it is **written** in the law of the Lord."* 2 Chron. 31:3

*"He did it with all his **heart**, and prospered."* 2 Chron. 31:21

The cry from the heart of God as it was in Jeremiah's day in 22:29 is still:

"O earth, earth, earth, hear the word of the Lord."

Response and Invitation

This Bible study manual was prepared as a ministry to Christians to help fulfill the Lord's great commission in discipleship: *"Teaching them to **observe all things** whatsoever I have commanded you,"* Matt. 28:20. And again, Acts 20:27, *"For I have not shunned to declare unto you all the counsel of God."*

Our vision concerning truth: that God will find men and women in His church who will never place a price tag on truth – they will refuse to sell truth no matter what the positive results might be. By His grace may we *"Buy the truth, and sell it not,"* Prov. 23:23.

My question to you regarding the hundreds of Scripture verses given in this manual concerning the church is not, did you enjoy it? Did you agree with it? Did you approve of it? Did you understand it? But, **What are you going to *do* about it?** This, in essence, is the response the Lord Jesus calls for at the end of His teaching, Matt. 7:24-27.

"Therefore whosoever heareth these sayings of mine, and doeth them, I will liken him unto a wise man, which built his house upon a rock: And the rain descended, and the floods came, and the winds blew, and beat upon that house; and it fell not: for it was founded upon a rock.

And every one that heareth these sayings of mine, and doeth them not, shall be likened unto a foolish man, which built his house upon the sand: And the rain descended, and the floods came, and the winds blew, and beat upon that house; and it fell: and great was the fall of it."

Matt. 7:24-27

If I can be of help in answering any questions on the truth presented, feel free to contact me at:

R.P. Amos
Box 331
Henrietta, N.Y. 14467

In the Love of Christ Jesus the Lord,

R.P. Amos